THE SWORD AND THE FLUTE

DAVID R. KINSLEY

The Sword and the Flute

KĀLĪ AND KṚṢṆA, DARK VISIONS OF THE TERRIBLE AND THE SUBLIME IN HINDU MYTHOLOGY

UNIVERSITY OF CALIFORNIA PRESS
BERKELEY, LOS ANGELES, LONDON

To the memory of my brother Roy

University of California Press
Berkeley and Los Angeles, California

University of California Press, Ltd.
London, England

First Paperback Edition, 1977
ISBN 0-520-03510-0
Library of Congress Catalog Card Number: 73-91669
Printed in the United States of America

2 3 4 5 6 7 8 9 0

CONTENTS

PREFACE

In September, 1968, I arrived in the teeming city of Calcutta to undertake research on the Bengal Vaiṣṇavas, those particularly enthusiastic worshipers of the Lord Kṛṣṇa. This research was part of my Ph.D. dissertation on play as an expression of the divine in the Hindu tradition. Kṛṣṇa, it seemed to me, was the perfect mythological expression of this idea, and it was with some eagerness that I anticipated seeing Kṛṣṇa expressing himself in a cultic context. I had come to India prepared to immerse myself further in the sublimely beautiful world of the flute-playing Lord of Vṛndāvana.

But September, October, and November in Bengal are the great festival months, and those deities that warrant the most dramatic, sumptuous, and tumultuous celebrations are goddesses, particularly Durgā and Kālī, both of whom reveal presences strikingly different from Kṛṣṇa's. First I was overwhelmed by Durgā Pūjā, that most joyous of all Bengali festivals in honor of the fierce, warrior goddess's triumph over the cosmic buffalo demon. Nearly a month later I was stunned by Kālī Pūjā, a tumultuous celebration of a fierce, female presence who haunts cremation grounds and on this occasion is actually worshiped publicly in them. On the last day of Kālī Pūjā I was invited to accompany some young men to the banks of the Hoogly River where the images of Kālī made especially for this festival are thrown into the murky waters. We set out for the river in an open truck, the image of Kālī facing backwards, braced against the rear of the truck's cab. There were perhaps twenty of us standing in the back of the truck trying our best to keep our balance in the lurching vehicle as it careened through the streets of Calcutta. The driver suddenly hit the brakes to avoid some obstacle, and I was thrown forward into the arms of Mother Kālī. Our first violent meeting broke one of her arms (I can't remember which of the four it was). I was embarrassed. I felt that perhaps I had made a particularly miserable blunder in breaking the goddess's arm. But I was assured by my friendly comrades that no harm had been done. The life of the image had been removed ritually prior to putting her on the truck, and she was really nothing much more now than a piece of clay. I was relieved. The next day, however, I caught a miserable cold that lasted for weeks. Where was Kṛṣṇa, I wondered?

In pursuit of Eden I had found something very different. Kṛṣṇa, of course, was there all the time, as beautiful and bewitching as I had thought he would be. But those first few months in Calcutta dramatically impressed upon me the fact that, for the Bengalis, at least, the divine reveals itself in terrible as well as sublime forms. This book, then, in which I have chosen to deal with two such strikingly different Hindu manifestations of the divine, is no accident. During that memorable year in Calcutta I began dabbling in the history and cult of Kālī while completing my research on Kṛṣṇa. It was, perhaps, in an oddly scholarly way, my way of doing obeisance to that presence I had so unceremoniously met in the back of a truck, my way of acknowledging that, although Kṛṣṇa's flute is symbolic of many central truths of the Hindu religious tradition, Kālī's sword is similarly symbolic and that perhaps there is an ultimate truth of the tradition that lies somewhere in an unimaginable combination of the two.

It has been my decision not to index this short work. The Contents page shows clearly and in some detail the scope of the book, with its two definite Parts and the division of its chapters into subject-matter headings. Important terms such as *ānanda*, *līlā*, and *prakṛti* can be located in these subtitles, and I believe that it would be useless to index "Kṛṣṇa" or "Kālī" or names like Balarāma or Rāmprasād.

INTRODUCTION

Blue lotuses
Flower everywhere
And black *kokilas* sing
King of the seasons,
Spring has come
And wild with longing
The bee goes to his love.
Birds flight in the air
And cowherd girls
Smile face to face
Krishna has entered
The great forest.[1]

Of terrible face and fearful aspect is Kālī the awful. Four-armed, garlanded with skulls, with disheveled hair, she holds a freshly cut human head and a bloodied scimitar in her left hands and makes the signs of fearlessness-assurance and bestowing boons with her right hands. Her neck adorned with a garland of severed human heads dripping blood, her earrings two dangling severed heads, her girdle a string of severed human hands, she is dark and naked. Terrible, fanglike teeth, full, prominent breasts, a smile on her lips glistening with blood, she is Kālī whose laugh is terrifying. Her flowing, disheveled hair streaming over her left side, her three eyes as red and glaring as the rising sun, she lives in the cremation ground, surrounded by screaming jackals. She stands on Śiva, who lies corpselike beneath her.[2]

Man has apprehended the divine in unbelievably varied and contrasting ways. The divine has revealed itself in sublime and terrible forms—in graceful, bounteous, merciful beings and in

[1]Vidyāpati, *Love Songs of Vidyāpati*, ed. W. G. Archer, trans. Deben Bhattacharya (London: George Allen & Unwin, 1963), no. 50, p. 89.

[2] The *dhyāna mantra* of Dakṣiṇa-kālī from Kṛṣṇānanda Āgamavāgīśa's *Tantrasāra* (*Bṛhat Tantrasārah*, 2 vols. [Calcutta: Basumatī Sāhitya Mandir, 1341 B.S. (1934)], 1:310–11). Kṛṣṇānanda is quoting from the *Śyāmā Praharaṇam.*

horrific, punishing, and wrathful deities. It has revealed itself, or been apprehended by man, in male, female, bisexual, androgynous, animal, plant, and geographical forms. The divine as revealed to man, or apprehended by him, has always shown the tendency to surprise, delight, and stun, to overpower man in ecstasy or overwhelm him with fear and trembling.

The Hindu religious tradition presents us with one of the richest and most diverse assemblies of divine beings to be found anywhere in man's religious heritage. The Hindu pantheon confronts us with a host of beings as varied and numerous as any in the world. The gallery of Hindu gods includes soft, beguiling deities, such as Lakṣmī and Pārvatī; withdrawn, ascetic gods, such as Śiva; kingly, active gods who involve themselves in maintaining the balance between good and evil, such as Viṣṇu and his assortment of incarnations; intoxicating and beautiful gods such as Kṛṣṇa; and terrible, frightening deities such as Kālī. There are innumerable regional and local gods and godlings, there are deities who assume theriomorphic disguises, and there are gods and goddesses who are primarily associated with mountains, rivers, cities, and pilgrimage sites.

The Hindu pantheon, because of its size and diversity, has sometimes proven an embarrassment to would-be defenders of the Hindu tradition, who are frequently reluctant to describe Hinduism as "polytheistic." The pantheon has also proven an embarrassment to orderly, scholarly minds who find difficulty in discerning neat, systematic patterns in the Hindu multitude of gods, godlings, and supernatural beings. The embarrassment (not shared by all, to be sure) is totally unwarranted. The very diversity and size of the Hindu pantheon testify eloquently to the fact that for the Hindu the divine cannot be circumscribed. The divine has consistently proven itself in the Hindu context so to transcend the finite world of man that it excites man's imagination to incredible and even extreme lengths in an attempt to apprehend it in its fullness.

Introduction

This study does not aim to discern an underlying system to the Hindu pantheon; it does not try to refute, affirm, justify, or condemn the term "polytheism" in the Hindu context. It tries, rather, to articulate the visions that underlie the mythologies and cults of two particularly popular Hindu deities, the god Kṛṣṇa and the goddess Kālī. In so doing, this study tries to convey the depth, complexity, and inexhaustible nature of the Hindu apprehension of the divine, the sacred, the holy, or the "other." It tries to emphasize the fact that in the Hindu tradition man has shown himself to be open to a divine dimension of reality that can both intoxicate and terrify him. It also tries to show that whether the divine delights or frightens it is ultimately redeeming to him who perceives it.

Certain methodological presuppositions should be made clear at the beginning. A primary presupposition of this study is the conviction that religious phenomena can best be understood on their own plane of reference. It is of course obvious that there is no such thing as a purely religious fact. Any religious phenomenon is also a social, psychological, and historical fact as well. This is the case because every religious phenomenon is, in the final analysis, also a *human* phenomenon, and the human phenomenon reveals itself in social, psychic, and historic milieus. This is all quite evident. What is not as obvious, perhaps, is that religious phenomena deserve to be interpreted in religious terms. They deserve to be interpreted for what they pretend to be—that is, manifestations (or revelations) of the sacred. Man is clearly a social, economic, and historical being. He is also, however, a religious being—a being who has traditionally demonstrated that he must relate himself to an "other" dimension of reality *in order to be human*. Religious things obviously meet social and psychic needs and fulfill certain social and psychic functions. Religious things clearly are also influenced by historical events. But religion also claims to transcend these "horizontal" factors, indeed, it claims to underlie these dimensions of reality.

Religion, as such, may be taken, and should be taken, as meaningful on its own plane of reference. The study of things religious can be first and foremost a study of *religious* man, a study of that dimension of man that he has consistently proclaimed to be the most ultimately real and the most ultimately human.

But how does one study religious things as religious things? This is not an easy question and does not elicit a simple answer. In the first place one does not study religion on its own plane of reference by ignoring what I have called "horizontal" factors. To understand religious things one must acquaint oneself with their contexts, one must be sensitive to the cultural setting of a given phenomenon. But what is more important one must seek to discern the visionary aspect of a religious phenomenon, that aspect of the phenomenon that legitimates it as a religious thing.[3] This means going beyond, or behind, the sometimes obvious social, psychic, or economic significance or function of a given phenomenon to grasp what the thing reveals to religious man, what the phenomenon reveals to man about that "other" realm of the sacred. This may call for a certain naïveté, a willingness to remain open to possibilities out of the ordinary, a willingness to marvel at and delight in the extraordinary—the willingness, perhaps, to wish that it might be so. One could say, it calls for one to be objective—for it prohibits the temptation to reduce a phenomenon to more easily manageable cause-and-effect interpretations. It does not allow one to foreclose any possibility

[3]The term *vision* is used here in a positive sense to denote man's apprehension of the real. Visions, as used here, are things that enable man to *see*—to see things as they really are. Visions enable men to see beyond the immediately sensed world of bits and pieces; they enable men to have a world, a cosmos. They situate man vis-à-vis an ultimate reality that grounds all else. Visions explode man out of his bound condition as a purely historical, and therefore limited, being and enable him to participate in a transcendent realm of "otherness." Visions impel man out of the ordinary and enable him to discern the extraordinary. Visions are not mere dreams, not hallucinations, but glimpses of something other that is ultimately meaningful to man.

but demands an openness to a dimension of reality that may not be experienced by the interpreter in his own life.

A second presupposition of this study stems from the first. When dealing with Kṛṣṇa and Kālī, with their mythologies and cults, we must seek interpretive directions from the larger religious tradition of which they are a part. Kṛṣṇa and Kālī are Hindu deities, and as such they undoubtedly reveal truths that are in some way related to, if not compatible with, other truths of this tradition. They are also very popular deities, particularly in Bengal. Their popularity suggests, further, that despite appearances (especially in the case of Kālī) they are not aberrations of the tradition but, quite likely, epitomes of or embroiderings on certain fundamental truths of the Hindu religious and philosophic traditions. It is my conviction that both deities do convey, in dramatic ways, central Hindu themes—that they articulate aspects of a primordial vision of the real that the Hindu tradition glimpsed thousands of years ago and that still underlies and orients the tradition today. This study tries to show how Kṛṣṇa and Kālī reveal and participate in that primordial vision.

This study is not historical in the sense of concerning itself primarily with chronicling the development of the Kṛṣṇa and Kālī cults. Particularly in the case of Kṛṣṇa, this task has already been done adequately by others.[4] In the case of Kālī, about whom very little has been done at all, this study is slightly more historical. It is primarily phenomenological, however. It seeks to bracket the phenomena under study in an attempt to apprehend a vision of reality that persists throughout

[4]For the history of Kṛṣṇa and the Kṛṣṇa cult, see William G. Archer, *The Loves of Krishna in Indian Painting and Poetry* (New York: Macmillan Co., 1957); R. G. Bhandarkar, *Vaiṣṇavism, Śaivism and Minor Religious Systems* (Varanasi: Indological Book House, 1966); Suvira Jaiswal, *The Origin and Development of Vaiṣṇavism* (Delhi: Munshiram Manoharlal, 1967); Hemchandra Raychaudhuri, *Materials for the Study of the Early History of the Vaishnava Sect* (Calcutta: University of Calcutta, 1936); and Charles S. J. White, "Kṛṣṇa as Divine Child," *History of Religions* 10, no. 2 (November 1970): 156-77.

the history of the two deities. This does not mean that the study dismisses the possibility of change resulting from historical developments in the Kṛṣṇa and Kālī cults. It is obvious that such change did take place—that both deities changed quite drastically, particularly in appearance and character. But change is interpreted in the study primarily as a modification, perhaps a clarification, of the primary visions that underlay the two deities. My approach is not to attempt to understand Kālī and Kṛṣṇa by amassing historical data: I seek instead to discern in the "presences" of these two beings, as revealed in history to be sure, hints of the transcendently real in the Hindu spiritual tradition. To put it in very unscholarly terms, my approach is to attempt to understand Kṛṣṇa and Kālī by trying to glimpse Kālī's sword and hear Kṛṣṇa's flute.

PART I

THE FLUTE: KṚṢṆA'S CARNIVAL OF JOY

CHAPTER I

Kṛṣṇa and "the Kṛṣṇas"

One of Hinduism's favorite gods, a god worshiped virtually throughout the entire subcontinent, is described as a youthful cowherd who lives in an idyllic forest setting. He is a surpassingly beautiful god who intoxicates and delights all those who see him or hear his flute. In the autumn, on full-moon nights, he beckons with his flute to his beloved cowgirl companions to join him in the forest, where they dance, sing, frolic, and make love with him. He wears a crown of peacock feathers, has a lovely blue complexion, and is an incorrigible prankster. He is Kṛṣṇa, the darling of Hindu devotionalism.

The Hindu tradition's "affair" with Kṛṣṇa has been varied and complex and has persisted for more than two thousand years. In the earliest stages Kṛṣṇa reveals himself primarily as a teacher, counselor, and friend. In the tradition's great epic, the *Mahābhārata*, he is the pivotal figure—the ally of the Pāṇḍava brothers in their struggle to regain their throne, which has been taken from them by the Kauravas. Throughout the vast epic Kṛṣṇa stands by the five warrior brothers, counseling and consoling them, acting as their diplomatic representative, and intervening at critical moments in the action in order to bring about eventual victory for his friends. His most famous and dramatic intervention has come to be known as the *Bhagavadgītā*, the "Song of the Lord," in which he reveals himself as an *avatāra* of Viṣṇu, an incarnation (or "descent") of the supreme god, whose divine purpose is to ensure victory for the just Pāṇḍavas. In this text Kṛṣṇa also reveals himself to be a skillful teacher, providing the Hindu tradition for millenia to come with a brilliant epitome of its most cherished teachings. Playing the role of Arjuna's charioteer (a humble and subservient role, like his later cowherd role),

Kṛṣṇa reveals himself in the *Gītā* as a divine being worthy of man's devotional love and service.

Not long after the final redaction of the *Mahābhārata* (circa 400 A.D.), and perhaps concomitant with it, the biography of Kṛṣṇa was elaborated in detail in the *Harivaṁśa* (the geneology of Hari, i.e., Kṛṣṇa), a text that was meant to be an appendix to the *Mahābhārata*. In the *Harivaṁśa* the details of Kṛṣṇa's birth and early life in a cowherd community (at Vraja or Vṛndāvana) are given, perhaps for the first time in the tradition.[1] It tells of his miraculous escape from his wicked uncle, Kaṁsa, his adoption by his foster parents, Nanda and Yaśodā, his pranks as a child, his play as an adolescent, and his love dalliance with the *gopīs* (cowherd women). These are episodes that eventually mark a transformation in the affair between Kṛṣṇa and the Hindu tradition, for the subsequent tradition becomes enamored of the cowherd youth, his mischievous childhood, and his passionate affair with the *gopīs*. The later tradition never entirely forgets the Kṛṣṇa of the epic—the loyal friend, political adviser, and teacher—but it becomes fascinated primarily by the gay and wild child of Vṛndāvana and dotes on him as a parent dotes on a child or as a woman dotes on her beloved, which is precisely the the context of the tradition's affair with Kṛṣṇa from this point onward.

In the *Viṣṇu-, Bhāgavata-, Padma-, and Brahma-vaivarta-purāṇas* the story of Kṛṣṇa's sojourn in Vṛndāvana is retold with increasing elaboration. In Jayadeva's *Gītāgovinda* (twelfth century A.D.) the complexities and subtleties of emotion involved in Kṛṣṇa's love affair with the cowherd women are explored in more depth with the appearance of Rādhā, Kṛṣṇa's favorite

[1]There is archaeological evidence for the cowherd Kṛṣṇa as early as the second century B.C. (Sukumar Sen, *A History of Brajabuli Literature* [Calcutta: University of Calcutta, 1935], p. 480), and the poet Bhāsa describes the child Kṛṣṇa (circa A.D. 200-300). The *Harivaṁśa*, however, even if it is later than the fourth century A.D., appears to be the first detailed account of Kṛṣṇa's childhood and youth.

beloved. In subsequent Vaiṣṇavite devotion, theology, philosophy, and poetry, Rādhā comes to take a central place, for she epitomizes the ecstatic, frenzied response of the Hindu tradition to the vision of the divine it has glimpsed in the divine youth Kṛṣṇa. In Rādhā the intoxication, passion, longing, and bliss of divine "madness" are dramatically and beautifully portrayed. In Kṛṣṇa mythology and cult she becomes the supreme paradigm of *prema*—selfless, passionate love for the beloved, the height of devotion to the divine.

It would be an exaggeration to say that in the history of Kṛṣṇa we have more than one Kṛṣṇa—a purely human hero (in the *Mahābhārata*), a divine incarnation (in the *Bhagavadgītā*), and the supreme god revealed as a cowherd youth (in the subsequent tradition). It would also be an oversimplification to interpret the history of Kṛṣṇa in the Hindu tradition along purely euhemerist lines.[2] It is apparent, nevertheless, that the Hindu tradition at a very early date bracketed Kṛṣṇa's childhood and youth—his dalliance in Vraja and Vṛndāvana—as the most sublime aspect of his biography or revelation. The Hindu tradition knows only one Kṛṣṇa, that eternal Lord who has revealed himself in so many ways, but it has also shown quite clearly its preference for particular aspects of Lord Kṛṣṇa's revelation. This study focuses upon those same aspects and attempts to discern and articulate the truths revealed in the beloved cowherd youth. In other words, in trying to grasp the central importance of Kṛṣṇa, this study follows the lead of the tradition by doting on Kṛṣṇa's life in Vṛndāvana. His earlier history will not be ignored. That would be to ignore the lesson of the tradition itself. But Kṛṣṇa's sojourn in Vṛndāvana will be the focus of the

[2]Euhemerist interpretations of Kṛṣṇa, in which he is supposed to be merely a human hero, invariably overlook his frequent superhuman feats in the *Mahābhārata* itself. It is impossible to read the *Mahābhārata* in its present form without sensing throughout that Kṛṣṇa moves against a background of divinity.

study, for it is in Vṛndāvana, the tradition has affirmed, that the divine has revealed itself most completely.[3]

The Divine Child: The Spontaneous and Tumultuous Nature of God

Perhaps the most obvious characteristic of the cowherd Kṛṣṇa, a characteristic that has clearly enamored the tradition of him, is his youth. Kṛṣṇa is the eternal child, the eternal adolescent and youth, whose pranks, uninhibited sporting, and wild gambols bear testimony, according to the Hindu tradition, to something essential in that other realm of the divine.[4] What does Kṛṣṇa's youth reveal about the divine, what do his revels tell us about the

[3] Although the *Bhagavadgītā* persists as unquestionably the most important Hindu scripture, Kṛṣṇa in the role of a teacher is very quickly overshadowed in the tradition by Kṛṣṇa the object of devotion. Even in the *Gītā* itself, Kṛṣṇa the teacher is overshadowed by Kṛṣṇa the Lord, to whom man should give his devotion. Mythically and devotionally the epic Kṛṣṇa in his role as counselor, charioteer, and confidant of the Pāṇḍava brothers is completely upstaged by Kṛṣṇa the cowherd. Later scriptures (e.g., the *Viṣṇu-* and *Bhāgavata-purāṇas*) do narrate Kṛṣṇa's later life, in which he takes part in the epic action, but they tell of it in less detail than of his childhood in Vṛndāvana. And, in the devotional movements of Vallabha and Caitanya, Kṛṣṇa's epic history is almost totally ignored. The later tradition does not deny Kṛṣṇa's epic roles. It remembers him, certainly, as the faithful ally and great teacher of the *Gītā*. But it looks elsewhere for his central significance.

[4] Just when the worship of the child Kṛṣṇa became popular is difficult to determine. The poet Bhāsa (third century A.D.) describes the child Kṛṣṇa, so it is clear this aspect of his biography was known at an early time. By the time of the South Indian Āḻvārs, sometime before A.D. 900, the baby god had clearly become the object of devotion. It is particularly in the North Indian Kṛṣṇa cults, however, that worship of Bāla Kṛṣṇa, the baby Kṛṣṇa, becomes overwhelmingly popular. In both the Vallabha and Caitanya sects, but especially in the former, worship of the child Kṛṣṇa is an important mode of approach to deity. The Hindi poet Sūrdās (1478–1581) was particularly partial to the baby Kṛṣṇa. As a member of the Vallabha sect he composed over eight hundred poems on the childhood of Kṛṣṇa. In the Caitanya sect of Bengal, although worship of the child Kṛṣṇa is practiced, Kṛṣṇa the lover is much more important. See White, "Kṛṣṇa as Divine Child."

Hindu vision of deity? Kṛṣṇa's life in Vṛndāvana as a youth, first of all, suggests the freedom and spontaneity of the divine.

In the form of a child, or more properly as a child, Kṛṣṇa behaves with utter spontaneity. He scrambles around the cowherd village with Balarāma, his elder brother, plays with his own shadow, rolls in the dust, dances to make his bangles jingle, eats dirt despite his mother's warning against it, laughs to himself, or sits quietly absorbed in his own imaginings. Kṛṣṇa the child passes his time in play, following every whim, acting without calculation, delighting the entire cowherd settlement. A few descriptions of the infant god will convey the freedom and spontaneity revealed in this theophany.

Kāhn [Kṛṣṇa] is joyfully crawling.
In Nanda's golden yard, studded with jewels, he is moving to catch his own image.
Looking at his shadow, sometimes he tries to grasp it with his hands.
He laughs gleefully and his two baby teeth shine; he wants to seize the reflection.

. . . .

Seeing the pleasant frolics of Kṛṣṇa, Yaśodā calls Nanda again and again.
Then, hiding Kṛṣṇa in the folds of her clothes she starts suckling him, says Sūrdās.[5]

The child Gopāla is dancing bewitchingly, and all the women of the Vraja are beating time with their hands and saying, "Fine, O really fine!" Nanda, Sunanda, Yaśodā and Rohiṇī are joyfully looking at the child's face. The red corners of his eyes are tinged with collyrium, and he shows his teeth when smiling.[6]

Looking like a child aged five years the Charmer (i.e., Young Kṛṣṇa) is romping about in the courtyard. (There is) sweet milk and butter, (which he) eats, and with which he smears his face. Ah, the graceful

[5]Surdas, "The Poems of Surdas," ed. and trans. S. M. Pandey and Norman H. Zide, mimeographed (Chicago: South Asia Language & Area Center, University of Chicago, 1963), poem 28.

[6]Vaṁśivadana-dāsa (sixteenth century); in Sen, *Brajabuli Literature*, p. 43.

swinging dance of the charming Gopāla . . . ! Quick are his steps, the girdle bells at his waist tinkle, and a garland of wild flowers . . . hangs down (from his neck). . . . Now he moves on tiptoe, and then he rolls on the ground: now he is gleeful, and then angry.[7]

The freedom and spontaneity of the child Kṛṣṇa are manifested particularly in his pranks. He has an insatiable appetite for butter and sweets and is constantly on the prowl in search of some to steal, thereby winning for himself the reputation of a notorious butter thief. In the *Bhāgavata-purāṇa,* where Kṛṣṇa seems first to have made his reputation as a butter thief, one of the *gopī* women comes to Yaśodā and complains of Kṛṣṇa's pranks. She accuses him of untying the calves, laughing when scolded, breaking pots to get butter, making infants cry, and relieving himself in freshly cleaned houses. The woman goes on to complain that, although Kṛṣṇa does all these things, he behaves as a perfect and obedient boy when near his mother.[8] In Jīva Gosvāmin's *Gopāla-campū* (sixteenth century A.D.) Kṛṣṇa and Balarāma are said to pretend to obey their mother until they are out of her sight, and then to do as they please.[9] And in the *Harivaṁśa* we are told that they are beyond Nanda's control.

They thus sported there like boys. . . . While they sported there they appeared like the sun and moon in the sky possessed by each other's rays. Going every where, they, having arms like serpents, appeared like two proud young elephants covered with dust. . . . Sometimes they used to walk on knees and enter cow-sheds and used to sport there with their persons and hairs covered with cow-dung. Sometimes committing mischiefs to the inhabitants of Vraja those two boys used to create the delight of their sire with their laughing. . . . They grew exceedingly

[7]Ghanarāma-dāsa (eighteenth century); ibid., p. 273.

[8]*Bhāgavata-purāṇa* X. 8. 26–31.

[9]Jīva Gosvāmin, *Śrī Śrī Gopāla-campū,* translated into Bengali by Rasabihāri Sāṁkhyatīrtha (Murshidabad: published under the patronage of the Rāja of Kasimbazar, Murshidabad, 1317 B.S. [1910]), p. 397.

playful and naughty and used to walk all over Vraja. And Nanda could not (by any means) check them.[10]

What is striking in these passages is that Kṛṣṇa's pranks and wildness, his disdain for convention, are not apologized for. The authors obviously approve of his mischief and enjoy flaunting it and elaborating on it. As an illustration of the spontancity and freedom of the divine, his pranks are perfectly in order.

Kṛṣṇa's pranks express an indifference to rules that typifies the behavior of children. The child's pranks and general misbehavior are not yet rebellion, as the child acts with little, if any, premeditation. The child has not yet assimilated social conventions and so is not yet limited by them. He behaves spontaneously, impetuously, without regard to "musts" and "oughts." The child seeks only to be amused and to amuse himself, and if such amusement means breaking parental or social rules, he goes right ahead and breaks them without hesitation. The child is free, that is, to express every impulse, to express his essential nature in every action.

The theophany of the child Kṛṣṇa, then, expresses the nature of the divine as unconditioned. God, like the child (in this case, as a child), belongs to a world that is not bound by social and moral convention, a world where fullness and bounty make work superfluous. For the divine to become embodied as a child is eminently suitable, for they behave in similar ways. Each belongs to a joyous realm of energetic, aimless, erratic activity that is pointless, yet significant: pointless, but at the same time imaginative and rich, and therefore creative. In play the mind can go wild; the imagination is set free to conjure and conquer. With the world of necessity left behind, the imagination takes over, eagerly populating a world that knows no limits whatsoever. So it is with the play of children, and so it is with the activity of

[10] *Harivaṁśa* 62. 3–12; *Harivamsha*, trans. Manmatha Nath Dutt (Calcutta: Elysium Press, 1897), p. 265.

the gods. The child Kṛṣṇa is by no means a partial, lesser manifestation of the divine in India. He epitomizes the nature and activity of the divine.

When Kṛṣṇa reaches adolescence he becomes the leader of a frolicking band of cowherd boys. They spend most of their time in the forests of Vṛndāvana gamboling in imitation of animals and playing games among themselves. They are no longer tied to their parents, and they create a world of their own, where Kṛṣṇa leads their play.

> They raced with the shadows of running birds. . . . They climbed in the branches of trees with young monkeys. . . . And plunged into the river with the jumping frogs. . . . Some laughed at their own reflections and jeered at the echo of their own voices.[11]

In the words of Jīva Gosvāmin, they created a "din and bustle" and behaved like "wildmen, roaming about aimlessly."[12] This band of cowherd boys is rarely still, as to be still or quiet is not the nature of youth. Their bodies and minds overflow with energy and enthusiasm, and the natural outlet for these is boisterous play. The following passages show their play to be charged with this irrepressible restlessness.

> After going to the forest, some of the young cowherds, like young elephants freed from their chains, began to dance, sing, laugh, and do acrobatic feats, while others expressed their happiness by simply rolling on the ground. Some of the boys joked, and others indulged in sports of various kinds.[13]

> With their heads as glossy black as the feathers of crows, Krishna and Balarama would sport by running, jumping, leaping, striking their

[11] Jīva Gosvāmin, *Gopāla-campū*, pp. 583–84.

[12] Ibid., pp. 541, 542.

[13] Kṛṣṇadāsa Kavirāja, *Govinda-līlāmṛta*, translated into Bengali by Saccidānanda Gosvāmin Bhaktiratna of Navadvīp (Vṛndāvana: printed under the patronage of Banamali Roy and published by Nityasvarup Brahmacāri at Śrī Daivokinanda Press, 1908), Sixth Sarga, p. 242.

arms with their hands, and tugging one another and wrestling amongst themselves.[14]

The play of the adolescent is similar to the play of the child and is often indistinguishable from it. The variety and complexity may be compounded, but the same carefree spirit pervades both. What is noteworthy about Kṛṣṇa's adolescent play is its wildness. Some of the descriptions of Kṛṣṇa and his group of friends sound like descriptions of a pack of wild young animals. They caper and gambol through the forest, and even imitate and play with animals. Their play is frivolous and merry, rollicking and free. In the *Harivaṃśa* Kṛṣṇa's play is said to be "like the fire in the cremation ground,"[15] leaping and flickering, erratic and vigorous.[16] The boastful, brash, and indomitable spirit of Kṛṣṇa's play makes the world around him sparkle with aliveness. His youthful play lights up the world around him as a blazing fire lights up the darkness. The playful actions of Kṛṣṇa and his companions burst forth to tumble and romp like the wind in the trees, unpredictable and free. We have here a description of that other realm where things are as they were meant to be, where life goes on joyously and unhampered, where no thought is given, or need be given, to the future, where life is lived to the fullest every moment. Kṛṣṇa's playful realm is a description of a heavenly world of the gods and a description of divine activity that is anarchical in its freshness and tumult. In his continuous sporting the happy adolescent Kṛṣṇa expresses the spontaneity

[14]*Bhāgavata-purāṇa* X. 18. 9; *The Srimad-Bhagavatam of Krishna-Dwaipayana Vyasa*, trans. J. M. Sanyal, vol. 4, 2d ed. (Calcutta: Oriental Publishing Co., n.d.), p. 84.

[15]*Harivaṃśa* 77. 35 (p. 324).

[16]A. K. Coomaraswamy, in fact, has suggested that the word *līlā*, "play," may derive from the root *lelay*, "to flare, flicker, or flame," and, even if *līlā* does not derive from this root, the association of ideas is clear, he adds, since both fire and play suggest spontaneous, erratic movement ("Līlā," *Journal of the American Oriental Society* 61 [1941]: 99).

and freedom of the divine in a way that is unique among Hindu gods.

If the theophany of the child god illustrates the spontaneous and tumultuous nature of the divine, it reveals a second aspect of deity just as clearly. As an infant and a child, Kṛṣṇa is approachable. Particularly as an infant (but also as an adolescent and lover) Kṛṣṇa is to be doted upon and coddled. He is to be approached with the intimacy with which a parent approaches a child. God, revealing himself as an infant, invites man to dispense with formality and undue respect and come to him openly, delighting in him intimately. The adorable, beautiful babe, so beloved by all the people of Vṛndāvana and by the entire Hindu tradition, does not demand servitude, pomp, and praise when he is approached. His simplicity, charm, and infant spontaneity invite an intimate, parental response like that shown by Nanda, Yaśodā, and the doting cowherd people of rustic Vṛndāvana.

The theophany of the child god also suggests a third aspect of deity—what might be called a transcendent aloofness from the world that arises from God's utter self-absorption and self-delight. God as an infant or child does not govern the world from a majestic throne. He shows little or no concern for world maintenance. He is completely absorbed in superfluous display and self-delight. The world is his playground or his plaything—something to enjoy but not be held responsible for. This is suggested clearly in a poem by the blind poet Sūrdās.

> Holding his foot in his hand, Gopāl is sucking his
> toe.
> He lies alone in his cradle absorbed in his happy
> play.
> Śiva has started worrying and Brahma has become
> thoughtful.
> The Banyan tree has reached the level of the water
> of the sea.
> Thinking that the clouds of Pralaya [cosmic disso-

lution] are gathering in the sky, the Dikpatis
are rounding up their elephants.
Sages are fearful in their hearts, the earth is
shaking and the serpent Śeṣa is spreading
his hood in anxiety.
The folks of Braj do not know what is happening.
Sūrdās says that he knows what will happen and
so is worried.[17]

God, as the baby Kṛṣṇa, is so absorbed in his own play that the world order has begun to run down. As this infant, God acts solely to amuse himself with no thought of the world. He feels no responsibility for the maintenance of the world and cares only to behave as he pleases. The infant god is a god who does not know work or responsibility, who passes his time in play. Worlds and universes, ultimately dependent on the child god, may come and go. The great gods may worry, the waters of cosmic dissolution may spread, the earth may shake because of the child god's self-absorption in his play. Aloof, absorbed in self-amusement and self-display, the child Kṛṣṇa is a testimony to a divine freedom and spontaneity that transcend the world order, a testimony to the essential nature of the divine as self-delight.

Kṛṣṇa's Sport with Demons: Combat as Play

Kṛṣṇa's carefree sojourn in Vṛndāvana is threatened from time to time by demons sent by his evil uncle Kaṁsa, who has learned of the child's whereabouts and has been forewarned that Kṛṣṇa will cause his downfall. But Kṛṣṇa's sole "purpose" in Vṛndāvana is carefree play and self-delight, and the horrendous demons sent to kill him not only are incapable of defeating the miraculous child but cannot even interrupt his superfluous gambols. The demons themselves simply become a new source of amusement

[17]Surdas, "The Poems of Surdas," poem 22.

for Kṛṣṇa. They are no match for him, and he disposes of them as if it were all a game. For the cowherd boy the slaying of these powerful beings is all in a day's play, as it were. Each time a demon makes an appearance in idyllic Vṛndāvana Kṛṣṇa dispatches him with ease and playful imagination.

The first fiend to be sent by Kaṁsa is the demoness Pūtanā, who disguises herself as a lovely woman. She dotes on the infant Kṛṣṇa and asks his mother if she may feed him from her own breasts. When Yaśodā allows her this privilege, Pūtanā poisons her nipples in an attempt to kill Kṛṣṇa. The poison, however, is ineffective, and the baby Kṛṣṇa turns the tables on the demoness by sucking the life from her.[18] The demon Trinavarta is the next victim. Sent by Kaṁsa, he appears in the form of a tumultuous whirlwind and sweeps the child into the air. Kṛṣṇa, however, becomes so heavy that the demon is barely able to keep aloft. Finally, nearly exhausted from bearing the weight of the child, he tries to drop his burden. Kṛṣṇa, however, clings tenaciously to the demon's neck, and Trinavarta, exhausted, falls to the ground like a rock, shattering himself.[19] Kṛṣṇa defeats the demon Batāsura, who appears in the guise of a calf, by hurling him by the tail into a tree.[20] When the demon Vakāsura, in the form of a huge crane, swallows Kṛṣṇa, the boy becomes so hot that the giant bird is forced to spit him out. Then Kṛṣṇa attacks the demon and "easily [tears] it into pieces like a twig."[21] Aghāsura, the younger brother of Pūtanā and Batāsura, assumes the form of a huge snake. Lying on the ground he opens his mouth, which covers the earth and reaches the sky. His fangs look like mountain peaks. The cowherd boys, mistaking the fiend for the presiding deity of Vṛndāvana, fearlessly enter its mouth and are

[18] *Bhāgavata-purāṇa* X. 6. 4–10 (4:25–26).

[19] Ibid., X. 7. 20–29 (4:31–32).

[20] Ibid., X. 11. 41–43 (4:46–47).

[21] Ibid., X. 11. 48–51 (4:47).

swallowed up. Kṛṣṇa rescues his friends by allowing the snake to swallow him too; once inside, Kṛṣṇa increases his size so that the creature is torn apart from within.[22] The demon Dhenuka, in the form of a giant ass, is killed by Balarāma. When Dhenuka's relatives come to the forest to avenge his death, they are handled easily by the two brothers.

Then Krishna and Balarama with perfect ease caught hold of these assaulting asses by their hind legs, and struck them against the palm trees. Then the ground of the forest was covered over with palm-fruits, palm twigs and the dead bodies of the Daityas (Dhenuka and his relatives) and resembled the beautiful firmament covered over with clouds.[23]

It is interesting to note that even the ground littered with the corpses of dead asses is not allowed to detract from the idyllic nature of Vṛndāvana. The sight of them, the author notes rather improbably, is as lovely as the cloud-filled sky! And the chopped-up corpse of the hag Pūtanā, when burned by the people of Vṛndāvana, gives off the sweet odor of sandalwood: the fiend was redeemed simply by her physical contact with Kṛṣṇa.[24]

To return to Kṛṣṇa's catalog of conquests: The petulant Iṅdra is humbled when he inflicts a torrential rainstorm on Vṛndāvana to chastise the cowherd people for neglecting him; Kṛṣṇa protects the people by holding Mount Govardhana aloft with his little finger for seven days as a huge umbrella.[25] The demon Ariṣṭa, disguised as a bull who shakes the earth with his strides, is also no match for the cowherd boy.

Kṛṣṇa stirred not from his post, but, smiling in sport and derision, awaited the near approach of the bull, when he seized him as an alligator

[22]Ibid., X. 12. 13–32 (4:49–51).

[23]Ibid., X. 15. 36–38 (4:70–71).

[24]Ibid., X. 6. 34 (4:28).

[25]Ibid., X. 25. 1–23 (4:108–10).

would have done, and held him firmly by the horns, whilst he pressed his sides with his knees.[26]

And so Ariṣṭa is crushed to death. The *asura* Keśī, in the form of a mighty horse, whose speed is as swift as the mind and whose neighs terrify the worlds, is simply tossed a distance by Kṛṣṇa. Regaining his senses, the stubborn Keśī attacks again. This time Kṛṣṇa thrusts his arm into the demon's mouth and increases its size until the demon chokes to death.[27]

Finally, in perhaps his most famous "battle" in Vṛndāvana, Kṛṣṇa defeats the many-headed serpent Kaliya. Kaliya lives in a nearby stream and has poisoned its waters, causing the death of many cattle. Kṛṣṇa arrives on the scene, surveys the situation, climbs into a tree, and leaps into the poisonous waters, where he begins to bait the monster by swimming and playing there. The enraged Kaliya emerges from his lair beneath the waters, and the battle begins. Kaliya seems to get the upper hand at first, gripping Kṛṣṇa in his coils. But Kṛṣṇa is only humoring him. Freeing himself from Kaliya's coils, he begins circling the demon until his heads begin to droop with exhaustion. Seeing his chance, Kṛṣṇa jumps onto the heads of the serpent and begins to dance. By rhythmically stamping his feet on the serpent's heads he tramples his enemy into submission. Battered and bloody from Kṛṣṇa's dancing, Kaliya finally admits defeat and seeks refuge in Kṛṣṇa's mercy. Kṛṣṇa, at the pleading of Kaliya's wives, grants him his life and banishes him to an island in the ocean.[28]

The mighty Kṛṣṇa, in the form of a child, is obviously invincible, and his contests with demons and fiends never pose any serious threat to him. He does not exert any measurable strength in these battles but, rather, toys with his adversaries. For the cow-

[26] *Viṣṇu-purāṇa* V. 14. 10–11; *The Vishṇu Purāṇa,* trans. H. H. Wilson, 3d ed. (Calcutta: Punthi Pustak, 1961), p. 427.

[27] *Bhāgavata-purāṇa* X. 37. 1–8 (4:150–51).

[28] Ibid., X. 16. 26–30 (4:75–76).

herd boy these "battles" are another form of play *(līlā)*, variations on his exercises in self-delight. Kṛṣṇa in Vṛndāvana cares nothing for the world of responsibility, of which the conquest of demons is a part. He does not go out of his way to defeat them, but if challenged by them he enters into the contest in a spirit of playful imagination. When a demon makes an appearance in the paradise of Vṛndāvana, Kṛṣṇa does not stop playing but continues his game right through the combat. The great player is not distracted from his play.

The Embodiment of Beauty and Grace

Another and obvious characteristic of the cowherd Kṛṣṇa is his surpassing beauty. Beauty is not an attribute of Kṛṣṇa alone. Many Indian gods are known for their beauty and grace. But Kṛṣṇa surpasses them all. He is the embodiment of that otherworldly grace, that astonishing divine beauty that transcends the ordinary world and attracts all who behold it. His every characteristic is the most beautiful, the most relishable. His speech is the most melodious and his conversation the wittiest.

> The speech of the Lord is sweet too. And it is full of much sweet humour. But the mischief that it does is unspeakable. For it enters by force the ears of all the maidens of the world. And by the cord of its sweetness it ties them all. And it pulls them so hard that the ears can hardly stand it.[29]

His smell is the most fragrant. One day in the forest when Kṛṣṇa became separated from his cowherd companions, they found him without difficulty simply by following his fragrant, irresistible

[29]Kṛṣṇadāsa Kavirāja, *Śrī Śrī Caitanya-caritāmṛta* (Bengali), 5 vols. (Calcutta: published by Mahoranjan Caudhuri at Sādhana Prākaśanī, 1963), Antya-līlā 15. 18; Krishnadasa Kaviraja Goswamin, *Sri Sri Chaitanya Charitamrita,* trans. Nagendra Kumar Ray, 2d ed., 6 vols. (Calcutta: Nagendra Kumar Ray, 1959), p. 261.

odor. "Then like bees attracted by the fragrance of flowers, they were attracted by the fragrance of Kṛṣṇa, and ran toward him in groups and touched him."[30] Even Kṛṣṇa's nails are worthy of comment and extolled in Vaiṣṇava scriptures.

> And the white nails in the hands of the Lord are also like so many moons. As the Lord blows His flute there, little moons dance upon the holes of the flute. They appear as if the tune proceeds not from the flute but from these beautiful nails of the Lord.
>
> And the nails of His feet are also like moons. They also seem to dance as the Lord walks and the tinkling sounds proceeding from the nupur (ornaments adorning the feet) appear to be songs sung by the moonlike nails.[31]

Kṛṣṇa's general appearance and every one of his features are subjects of endless poetic descriptions. His appearance is redeeming in itself and so is invoked in nearly every Vaiṣṇava-Kṛṣṇa text. Over and over again we read of his luminous dark complexion, large dark eyes, black curly hair, gleaming white teeth, and full lips. For devotees of Kṛṣṇa the image of their blue lord is the quintessence of divine beauty. The *Brahma-vaivarta-purāṇa,* a fairly late Vaiṣṇava work, describes Kṛṣṇa as emanating a blinding light adored by mystics and *yogins.* But Kṛṣṇa's devotees see within that dazzling light to the even more dazzling and redeeming image of their darling.

> But the Vaiṣṇavas adore the indescribable, lovely image of Kṛṣṇa located in the centre of this light. He is blue like a new cloud; his eyes are like lotuses; his face is as graceful as the autumnal full Moon; his lips are like *bimbas*; the row of his teeth shames the pearls. A gentle smile plays on his lips. He holds a flute in his hands. . . . He is clad in yellow dress.[32]

[30] Jīva Gosvāmin, *Gopāla-campū*, p. 582.

[31] Kṛṣṇadāsa Kavirāja, *Caitanya-caritāmṛta*, Madhya-līlā 21. 107 (p. 535).

[32] *Brahma-vaivarta-purāṇa*, Brahma Khanda 21. 32 ff.; *Brahma-Vaivarta Pura-*

The charming cowherd youth of Vṛndāvana, the lively, rambunctious, lithe adolescent, is not merely a form of the divine for Kṛṣṇa devotees. This dark youth in yellow dress who sports a peacock feather for a crown *is* the divine, the divine in its unadulterated form, in its essential nature *(svabhāva)*. As such the youth is absolutely irresistible, hypnotizing in his appearance. The famous sixteenth-century poetess Mīrābāī, an impassioned devotee of Kṛṣṇa, whom she proclaimed to be her husband, conveys the attraction of Kṛṣṇa in lovely imagery.

As in summer blooms a garden so my spirit buds and blooms; and of every flower the name is always Krishna. As a butterfly in sunshine filled with light in blue air hovers thus I dance. In the golden halls of Brindaban I dance before my Krishna on whose brow gleams the Tilakam. Holy Krishna. From my lips I tear concealment and my willing breasts reveal; love inflamed I dance into the Light of Blessed Krishna![33]

So it is in almost every Vaiṣṇava-Kṛṣṇa work. The physical appearance of Kṛṣṇa is doted upon and affirmed as redeeming in itself. And the ultimate goal of all devotees is actually to see Kṛṣṇa in a vision while living or to dwell with him in heavenly Vṛndāvana after death. The attitude of the devotee should be like that of the *gopī* who cursed the creator for having given her eyelashes that prevented her from seeing Kṛṣṇa constantly.[34]

Kṛṣṇa's beauty is not limited strictly to his own physical appearance. It pervades his dwelling place *(dhāman)* and those who live there with him (particularly the cowherd people of

---

nam, trans. Rajendra Nath Sen (Allahabad: Sudhindra Nath Vasu), part 1: *Brahma and Prakriti Khandas* (1920), part 2: *Ganesa and Krishna Janma Khandas* (1922), 1:65.

[33]Paul Althaus, *Mystic Lyrics from the Indian Middle Ages*, trans. P. Althaus (London: George Allen & Unwin, 1928), p. 34.

[34]Kṛṣṇadāsa Kavirāja, *Caitanya-caritāmṛta,* Madhya-līlā 21. 112 (p. 534).

Vṛndāvana). Vṛndāvana and its inhabitants are extensions of Kṛṣṇa's nature and as such also convey the beauty, grace, and charm of the dark lord. Kṛṣṇa devotees know Vṛndāvana as the ultimate goal of their spiritual quest. Although Vṛndāvana is considered simply the temporary home of Kṛṣṇa during his youth in such early Vaiṣṇava scriptures as the *Harivaṁśa, Viṣṇu-purāṇa,* and *Bhāgavata-purāṇa,* by the time of the *Brahma-vaivarta-purāṇa* it has become identified with the highest heaven.[35] Beyond Śiva's Mount Kailasa, beyond the far-off place where Brahman meditates in stillness, even beyond Viṣṇu's heavenly Vaikuṇṭha, beyond the reach of the imagination, suspended in space by the will of Kṛṣṇa, is the highest heaven, and it is nothing else but the idyllic forest town of Vṛndāvana unabashedly magnified. Just as Kṛṣṇa in the form of the beautiful adolescent cowherd came to attain the supreme position as the highest god, Bhagavān, so his earthly sporting ground, the humble Vṛndāvana, came to attain the place as the highest heaven.

Within the spherical light . . . of that mighty corporeal Being [Kṛṣṇa], there exists a region called the Goloka, or the Cow-world, quadrangular, covert and expanded over an area of 9 lakh crores of miles. This region is very lovely and round like the Moon, built with precious gems and suspended on the void by the will of God, without any support. It is situated 50 crores of Yojans above the Vaikuṇṭha. It is full of cows, cow-herds, cow-herdesses and Kalpa-trees, teems with celestial cows which fulfil all desire, is decorated with the sphere of the Râsa . . .

[35]J. N. Farquhar thinks this work is a product of the Nimbārka school, tenth to eleventh centuries (*An Outline of the Religious Literature of India* [Delhi: Motilal Banarsidass, 1967], pp. 240, 271, 376). S. K. De (*Early History of the Vaisnava Faith and Movement in Bengal from Sanskrit and Bengali Sources* [Calcutta: Firma K. L. Mukhopadhyay, 1961], p. 11) is not willing to guess which sect produced it but says that it was probably contemporaneous with Jayadeva, end of the twelfth century. F. S. Growse suggests that the Bengal Gosvāmins of Vṛndāvana may have composed it in the sixteenth century (*Mathura: A District Memoir* [n.p.: North-Western Provinces & Oudh Government Press, 1883], p. 75).

and encompassed by the wilderness of Vrindâ-Vanâ. It is surrounded by the river Virajâ, decorated by the hundred summits of the Śata-Sringa mountains and ornamented with millions of hermitages possessing countless mansions.[36]

Because Kṛṣṇa's heavenly sporting ground is identical with the scene of his earthly life as a youth, all his earthly sports continue there too, only eternally. In that high heaven Kṛṣṇa plays as a child, steals butter, romps with his young friends, plays his flute, and dallies with the *gopīs*. In fact, what happens in earthly Vṛndāvana is simply a reflection of what happens continually in heavenly Vṛndāvana. The translation of the cowherd settlement into the loftiest divine sphere underlines the fact that the divine for Kṛṣṇa devotees is coincident with beauty and grace, for heavenly Vṛndāvana is preeminently a place of bountiful natural beauty and elegant grace.

The heavens of the other Hindu gods are also lovely places and are populated by teeming bands of *apsarases, siddhas,* and *gandharvas*—lovely, lithe creatures who sing, dance, and entertain the deity. But Vṛndāvana more than any other place is noted for its extraordinary beauty. The fact that heavenly Vṛndāvana does not have *apsarases, gandharvas,* and *siddhas* does not detract in any way from its beauty, for in that charmed place live thousands of young cowherd boys and girls who fulfill the same functions. While other gods and other heavenly beings appear in Vṛndāvana on certain occasions, to watch and applaud Kṛṣṇa's fights with demons, to watch his *rāsa* dance with the *gopīs*, or in answer to his flute, it is the *gopas* and *gopīs* who are the main guardians of Kṛṣṇa's sport. It is they who are primarily responsible for maintaining it and participating in it. They sing, dance, play, and revel in erotic dalliance just as the heavenly nymphs do. In fact, these humble people portrayed in the *Purāṇas are* heavenly nymphs in Kṛṣṇa's heaven.

[36] *Brahma-vaivarta-purāṇa,* Brahma Khaṇḍa 28. 40–46 (1:79).

> Kṛṣṇa sang songs composed in poetic verse and began to dance with the playful and witty women of Vrāja. When he began to dance with Rādhā, Lalitā and other *sakhīs* [female friends and companions of Rādhā and Kṛṣṇa] began to sing, Chitra and others kept time by clapping their hands, and Brida and others looked on, judging the merit of the songs and dances. The rest of the women sang songs and played on harps and other instruments while surrounding the dancers like a protective screen. The sounds of harps, gongs, flutes, drums, and singing blended in harmony. The women kept time with their feet. All their bodily movements were in tune with the music there in that playground with Kṛṣṇa.[37]

In early Vaiṣṇava *Purāṇas* the *gopīs* are portrayed as rustic women who live in the country, tend cows, and churn butter. In later Vaiṣṇava-Kṛṣṇa literature, such as the *Brahma-vaivarta-purāṇa* and the *Govinda-līlāmṛta,* however, most of their rough edges have been polished. They are first and foremost Kṛṣṇa's playmates, and their primary function is to amuse him and be amused by him. As such they have become accomplished concubines who excel at singing and dancing.

> The women who had been playing on harps and flutes now began to sing and provided the background music for the dance, while those women who had been playing drums joined the dancers and danced with great pleasure. Carried away with dancing and singing their hair and clothes came unfastened, so Kṛṣṇa stopped the dance and retied them again. The women sang again using all the musical scales. They sang in pure and mixed *rāgas*, and sang thousands of tunes in both the classical and popular styles. Their songs, accompanied by gongs, sounded like the deep rumbling of the clouds in the rainy season. . . . The male dancer was Kṛṣṇa, and the female dancers were the fair women of Vraja. The mingled sounds of their bracelets, anklets, and earrings formed the height of musical delight. As they danced the women sang, their hands made gestures expressing their moods, their lotus feet beat time, their bodies trembled in dance, and their eyes followed Kṛṣṇa.

[37]Kṛṣṇadāsa Kavirāja, *Govinda-līlāmṛta*, pp. 1261–62.

Their delight in being near Kṛṣṇa was reflected in his face, and they were thus further inspired.[38]

In the *Brahma-vaivarta-purāṇa* the husbands and children of the *gopīs* are rarely mentioned. The *gopīs* never work but spend all their time accompanying Rādhā to her trysting place, entertaining Kṛṣṇa, or romping with Kṛṣṇa all over his heaven.

The milk-maids having wantonly played with Hari in the sphere of the Râsâ played with him again on different occasions and in different places, in some lovely solitary place, in a grove of flowers, on the coast of a river, in the cave of a mountain, in a crematorium, in the forest of the holy fig tree, in the Vrindâvana, in the pleasing forest of the Kadam, in the forest of Nim.[39]

The *gopīs* stage plays and prove themselves to be accomplished actresses. And they particularly enjoy imitating Rādhā and Kṛṣṇa.

Some of the girls with pitchers on their head were dancing. Some of them were dressed as males and others played the parts of heroines courted by the above males. Some assumed the form of Râdhâ: and others, of Kṛṣṇa. Some mixed freely with others. Some were embracing their companions: others were playing.[40]

Although the *gopīs* are not supernatural beings who fly through the air like the celestial *apsarases* and *siddhās*, they are just like them in almost every other respect. In these late Vaiṣṇava-Kṛṣṇa passages the *gopīs* are no longer simple country women faithfully carrying out their domestic routines. They are talented and impish playmates of Kṛṣṇa who adorn his heaven with grace and beauty.

[38]Ibid., pp. 1270–71.

[39]*Brahma-vaivarta-purāṇa,* Kṛṣṇa Janma Khaṇḍa 28. 159–63 (2:234–35).

[40]Ibid., 4. 79–81 (2:113).

Another aspect of Vṛndāvana that emphasizes the grace and harmony of Kṛṣṇa's world is the popularity of dancing in Vṛndāvana. This has already been seen in many of the passages cited earlier, but I would like to comment specifically on Kṛṣṇa as a dancer and the importance of dance in his realm. Kṛṣṇa dances rhythmically when he plays in his mother's courtyard as a child, he dances in the forest with his young companions, he defeats the serpent Kaliya by dancing on his heads, he dances with Rādhā, and he dances collectively with the *gopīs* in the *rāsa* dance. Through his dancing, Kṛṣṇa expresses his exquisite charm and grace. In the *Purāṇas* and later Vaiṣṇava-Kṛṣṇa texts he no longer retains any of the sharp, caustic features of the epic counselor and politician. His bearing is not impressive in its nobility but gentle in its beauty. His figure is lithe and his movements fluid. And he displays this constantly in dance, in superfluous motion.

Syama, who delights in the sport of *Rāsa*, and who is a young prince, (is dancing) in the company of young damsels. He is moving in quick steps to charming music. He dances in charming steps and with delightful movements of the body. Lutes and other musical instruments are being played to accompaniment. Drums *(mṛdaṅga)* are raising a beautiful note—*tā tā, thai thai, thai.* Kānu raises a charming music with his lovely anklets, and he is singing a fine melody in proper beats and harmony.[41]

Because he is the embodiment of grace and joy, Kṛṣṇa's every gesture and movement is rhythmic and harmonious. In the *Dāna-keli-kaumudī* he is described as "coming down from the top of the mountain [to meet the *gopīs*] dancing all the while."[42] Indeed, some Vaiṣṇava writers have said that the movements of all inhabitants of Vṛndāvana are so graceful that they are dance-

[41]Śivarāma-dāsa; in Sen, *Brajabuli Literature*, p. 178.

[42]Rūpa Gosvāmin, *Dāna-keli-kaumudī*, translated into Bengali by Rāmanārāyaṇa Vidyāratna (Murshidabad: published by Brājanāth Misra at Rādhā-ramaṇ Press, 1339 B.S. [1932]), p. 48.

like and their voices so melodious that their speech is like song. "Pleasing song is the natural speech of the people there, and their natural gait is dance."[43] In the heavenly sporting ground of Kṛṣṇa's paradise, ordinary things such as walking and speaking lose their pragmatic nature altogether and become dance and song. For this is where Kṛṣṇa is. And where Krsna is, nothing is ordinary, nothing is harsh, nothing is graceless.

Vṛndāvana, finally, as Kṛṣṇa's dwelling place, reflects his irresistible beauty in its own natural beauty, which is exquisite and which Vaiṣṇava writers seem never to tire of describing. Indeed, lengthy tracts have been written for the sole purpose of praising its virtues and proving it to be the supreme paradise. Prabodhānanda Sarasvatī was particularly fond of describing Vṛndāvana and set himself the task of writing ten thousand verses on this single theme.[44]

I have been enchanted by the flora of Vṛndāvana, the strangely beautiful, varied trees and fruit- and flower-bearing creepers; by the calls and songs of beautiful peacocks, cuckoos, parrots, and other birds, their songs maddened by bliss; by lakes surrounded by green bowers; by the rivers and mountains. The golden fields of Vṛndāvana have also captured me. In Vṛndāvana the earth is made of transparent stones and gems of various kinds. Its trees and creepers are laden with flowers and fruits that diffuse bliss. Birds sing the sweetest songs of the *Sāma-veda*. The waters of rivers, lakes, and tanks are full of *rasa* of pure consciousness. Let my mind ponder them! The leaves are like emeralds in Vṛndāvana, the flowers are like diamonds, the sprouts and fruit are like rubies, while the trees in Vṛndāvana stand picturesquely with perpetually honey-shedding flowers, and the flowers are covered with large, black bees that look like shining blue gems.[45]

[43] Kṛṣṇadāsa Kavirāja, *Caitanya-caritāmṛta,* Madhya-līlā 14. 211.

[44] De, *Vaisnava Faith and Movement,* p. 653. He did not accomplish his goal but did complete 1,871 verses.

[45] Prabhodhānanda Sarasvatī, *Vṛndāvana-mahimāmṛta,* translated into Bengali by Haridās Babaji (Vṛndāvana: Bhagavāndās Babaji, 1936), part 2, pp. 1–2.

And on and on. In Vṛndāvana, nature itself seems to revel in bliss, intoxicated by Kṛṣṇa and intoxicating all the inhabitants of Kṛṣṇa's celestial paradise in return. In Vṛndāvana the extremes of heat and cold are not known. During the time of the insufferable summer heat, spring continues to reign in the forest town.[46] In Kṛṣṇa's heaven naturally hostile animals are friendly to each other.[47]

Finally, in Vṛndāvana no one knows old age or death.

> Vṛndāvana, the abode of his love-games, is beyond description; it is self-luminous, and consists in love and joy. There happiness reigns, and in that land of infinite bliss there is no old age, nor death nor pain. There the relishful love-games of Krishna go on without cease.[48]

Kṛṣṇa is eternally young in Vṛndāvana, and so are all of its inhabitants. Nature does not wear them down but constantly expresses her joy through youthful vigor. The wheel of life and death does not revolve in Kṛṣṇa's heaven. It has permanently stopped to revel in life alone, entranced, as it were, by Kṛṣṇa's bewitching presence.

The Call of Kṛṣṇa's Flute

Kṛṣṇa's flute is an extension of his beauty. Not only is it the most beautiful sound imaginable, but it also imparts the essence of Kṛṣṇa's intoxicating nature. While Kṛṣṇa is also adept at singing, it is the sound of his flute, not his voice, that echoes throughout Vṛndāvana, beckoning all to join him in the forest.

The flute is perhaps the simplest of musical instruments, a mere hollow stick, and this permits Kṛṣṇa to express himself through

[46] *Bhāgavata-purāṇa* X. 18. 3 (4:83).

[47] Ibid., X. 13. 60 (4:57–58).

[48] Krishnadas [Charuchandra Guha], *Krishna of Vrindabana* (Calcutta: Bengal Library Book Depot, 1927), p. 596.

it with a minimum of adulteration. The flute gives forth a clear, pure, simple sound that can be both intensely melancholy and entrancingly sprightly. In either mood, haunting or haughty, its clear notes sound as if they come from a world beyond the din of the ordinary. Amid the sounds of the humdrum world, the flute, especially Kṛṣṇa's flute, is sweet and pure, prancing along to nowhere in particular. It comes from and belongs to that world of abundance and bliss that Kṛṣṇa rules.[49]

The sound of Kṛṣṇa's flute, though, is more than a melody. It is a summons, a call to come to him. It calls the souls of men back to their Lord.

> The lute stands for the attractive power of Kṛṣṇa. . . . It is a part of his Divine Sport that he unfolds himself into diversity involving

[49]The following anecdote makes the same point, and, although it reminds Ortega y Gasset of the god Pan, it bears striking similarities to Kṛṣṇa and his flute. Ortega y Gasset is reminiscing about his childhood and a circus he once attended.

> A clown would stroll in with his livid, floured face, seat himself on the railing, and produce from his bulky pocket a flute which he began to play. At once the ringmaster appeared and intimated to him that here one could not play. The clown, unperturbed, stalked over to another place and started again. But now the ringmaster walked up angrily and snatched his melodious toy from him. The clown remained unshaken in face of such misfortune. He waited till the ringmaster was gone, and plunging his hand into his fathomless pocket produced another flute and from it another melody. But alas, inexorably, here came the ringmaster again, and again despoiled him of his flute. Now the clown's pocket turned into an inexhaustible magic box from which proceeded, one after another, new musical instruments of all kinds, clear and gay or sweet and melancholy. The music over ruled the veto of destiny and filled the entire space, imparting to all of us with its impetuous, invincible bounty a feeling of exultation, as though a torrent of strange energies had sprung from the dauntless melody the clown blew on his flute as he sat on the railing of the circus. Later I thought of this clown of the flute as a grotesque modern form of the great god Pan of the forest whom the Greeks worshipped as the symbol of cosmic vitality—serene, goat-footed Pan who plays the sacred syrinx in the sinking dusk and with its magic sound evokes an echo in all things: leaves and fountains shiver, the stars begin to tremble, and the shaggy goats dance at the edge of the grove.

(José Ortega y Gasset, *Toward a Philosophy of History* [New York: W. W. Norton & Co., 1941], pp. 20–21.)

the plurality of individual souls. But it is a part of the same Sport that he calls the souls back to his own self.[50]

The nature of the call, consistent with the nature of Kṛṣṇa, is irresistibly charming. In this poem its enchanting sound is called the "All-pervading Net," from which no person or thing is immune:

". . . The pipe (he plays on) is by nature contrary, and it is known to all the world by the name of the 'All-pervading Net': at the guidance of Kānu it is wantonly cruel, and it is a veritable enchanting maze for girls. Neither faults nor virtues does it count; nor does it respect time or duty." The Lord of Rāya Vasanta is an enchanter: can there be in him any consideration for others?[51]

The call of Kṛṣṇa's flute is anarchical, breaking down and mocking resistance. And the best way to convey its entrancing nature is to give some examples of its effects on those who hear it. The Vaiṣṇava scriptures and poems delight in describing the effect of Kṛṣṇa's flute on the *gopīs*, who are all married women but are powerless to resist its call. A famous passage from the *Bhāgavata-purāṇa* expresses this well.

Beholding the friend of the lilies (moon) rise in his full splendour on the sky, and shine like the countenance of (Lakshmi), red like fresh saffron, and also seeing the groves flooded and variegated with the soft lustre of the moon, Krishna melodiously sang with his flute in a manner so as to captivate the hearts of women with beautiful eyes.

Having heard that music capable of exciting desire, the damsels of Braja had their heart[s] enslaved by Krishna. Without apprising one another of their respective intentions, they (the *Gopees*) hastened to the place where their darling was. Their ear-rings dangled on account of their haste. Some damsels who had been milking their cows, started anxiously leaving the milking half-done. Some went away leaving

[50]Siddheśvara Bhaṭṭācārya, *The Philosophy of the Śrīmad-Bhāgavata* (Santiniketan: Visva-Bharati), vol. 1: *Metaphysics* (1960), vol. 2: *Religion* (1962), 1:116.

[51]Rāya Vasanta (sixteenth century), in Sen, *Brajabuli Literature*, p. 142.

the milk they had been boiling over fire, without waiting for its boiling. Others again flew to him (Krishna), without even taking down, from the hearth, the preparation of wheat they had been baking. Some had been distributing eatables among [their] family members, some had been suckling their babies, some had been taking their meals, some had been toileting with cosmetics, some had been cleansing their persons and some had been painting their eyes with collyrium. All those *Gopees*, leaving their respective business and duties unfinished flew to Krishna their garments and ornaments having fallen off their persons in consequence of their great hurry.[52]

In the *Gītāgovinda* the effect of Kṛṣṇa's flute is described as being similarly bewitching.

> Hear the maddening flute-born melody
> Of the Enemy of Madhu dance
> On the air; it captivates the free
> Maidens with its magic spell in trance.[53]

The Bengali poet Govinda-dāsa, finally, describes the helpless *gopīs* all aflutter when they hear Kṛṣṇa's flute and recalls the passage from the *Bhāgavata-purāṇa*.

(It is) an autumnal moon; a soft wind (is blowing); the woodland is saturated with the perfume of flowers; *mallikā, mālatī,* and *yūthī* flowers (are) in bloom, (and they are) deceiving the bees. On seeing such beauty of the night Śyāma, intoxicated with the charm of love, (begins) to play the fifth note *(pañcama tāna)* that steals the hearts of chaste girls. The *Gopīs* hear it and they are filled with love. Mentally they offer themselves (to Kṛṣṇa) and run to the place from where issues the passionate music of the flute. They forget their home; they forget their body. (Some have) painted with collyrium only single eyes; some girls' single arms only are decked with bracelets; and some have only single earrings dangling. The knots of their girdles have become loosened.

[52] *Bhāgavata-purāṇa* X. 29. 3–7 (4:119–20).

[53] Jayadeva, *Gītāgovinda* 11. 20. 3; Jayadeva, *The Song of Divine Love (Gita-Govinda)*, trans. Duncan Greenlees (Madras: Kalakshetra Publications, 1957), p. 74.

The maidens are rushing on with speed; their clothes and girdles are slipping away (from their person), and their top-knots, becoming loose, dangle at their back. Then the friends meet, but they cannot take any notice of each other on the way. In this manner they came to the Moon of Gokula (*i.e.*, Kṛṣṇa). So sings Govindadāsa.[54]

The flute's effect on Rādhā is even more tumultuous and alarming, and this is another favorite theme of Vaiṣṇava writers. In a poem by the seventeenth-century Bengali poet Vrāja-kiśora, Rādhā is described as so distracted by the flute that she cannot dress herself properly.

Rādhā was dressing herself (for going out) when the flute sounded, and it did not stop. (Rādhā's) heart was overwhelmed with love: she lost control over her actions. Her heavy tresses, already done, she combs (again): she ties the wreath of flowers round her leg; she has lost all consideration. Her feet she paints with collyrium, and her eyes with red-dye. She pushed *nāga-latā* into the cavities of her ears. The girdle she puts on her neck, the necklace round her waist: the anklets she fastens round her wrists and wristlets round her ankles. Being thus intoxicated (as it were), Rāï walks quickly away. Why indeed does not the cruel way end soon? Vraja-kiśora says: the path ended (at last) and reaching Nidhuvana Rāï raised a cry of joy.[55]

In the following two poems the effect of the flute is violent in its intensity. Rādhā is "thrust to the ground" and speaks of women being dragged by their hair to the forest.

At the first note of his flute
down came the lion gate of reverence for elders,
down came the door of *dharma*,
my guarded treasure of modesty lost,
I was thrust to the ground as if by a thunderbolt.
Ah, yes, his dark body

[54]Govinda-dāsa Kavirāja, in Sen, *Brajabuli Literature,* p. 125.

[55]Vrāja-kiśora, in ibid., pp. 417–18.

poised in the *tribhanga* pose[56]
shot the arrow that pierced me;
no more honor, my family
lost to me,
my home at Vraja
lost to me.
Only my life is left—and my life too
is a breath that is leaving me.
So says *Jagadānanda-dāsa*.[57]

How can I describe his relentless flute,
which pulls virtuous women from their homes
and drags them by their hair to Shyām
as thirst and hunger pull the doe to the snare?
Chaste ladies forget their lords,
wise men forget their wisdom,
and clinging vines shake loose from their trees,
hearing that music.
Then how shall a simple dairymaid withstand its call?
Chandidāsa says, Kālā the puppetmaster leads
the dance.[58]

The call of Kṛṣṇa's flute cares nothing for this world and its moral and social laws. It comes crashing in upon man and cannot be denied. It comes from another world where this-worldly morality and conduct have no place. Nothing in this world is able to keep Rādhā or the *gopīs* from answering its call.[59] The

[56]*Tribhanga* is "thrice bent." This is Kṛṣṇa's most famous pose, in which he is bent at the waist, at the neck, and at the knee, with one leg crossed over the other. It is a very graceful posture and is typical of Kṛṣṇa the "dandy." The pose may be seen in any book dealing with the Kṛṣṇa legend in Kangra painting.

[57]Edward C. Dimock and Denise Levertov, trans., *In Praise of Krishna: Songs from the Bengali* (Garden City, N.J.: Doubleday & Co., 1967), p. 28.

[58]Ibid., p. 29.

[59]The debate that took place in Bengal Vaiṣṇavism concerning whether Rādhā and the *gopīs* were Kṛṣṇa's wives *(svakīyā)* or the wives of others *(parakīyā)* serves to underline this point. In the *Bhāgavata-purāṇa* it is fairly clear that the *gopīs* were the wives of others, but this did not deter Rūpa and Jīva Gosvamīn from

flute calls them to a world of ravishing beauty, boisterous carnival, and rollicking play that makes the ordinary world look pale, unexciting, and wearisome by comparison.

Even the gods cannot ignore the sound of Kṛṣṇa's flute. Their heavenly abodes seem dull compared to Kṛṣṇa's luscious Vṛndāvana, and so when Kṛṣṇa plays his flute the celestials are irresistibly drawn also. The heavenly maidens "lose all patience and become senseless";[60] the gods "hearing those harmonious cadences lose consciousness [and] bend their necks and concentrate their hearts, to catch the music all the better."[61]

> The sound of the Lord's flute suddenly diffused all over; it astonished the clouds; it struck wonder into the hearts of *Tumburu* and other *Gandharvas*; it cried halt to the hearts of Sananda and other sages deep in their meditation. It astonished the Lord Brahma, augmented the holy exultation of the king *Vali*. And last not the least of all, it made the head of the Ananta, king of the serpents [the primordial foundation

trying to prove the opposite. Their argument is primarily theological and revolves around the idea that, since the *gopīs* and Rādhā are really manifestations of Kṛṣṇa's *svarūpa-śakti*, they are *svakīyā*, not *parakīyā*, to him. Rūpa even went so far as to portray a regular marriage between Rādhā and Kṛṣṇa in the tenth act of his play *Lalitā-mādhava* (translated into Bengali by Satyendranāth Basu [n.p.: published by Satiścandra Mukherji at Basumati Sāhitya Mandir, n.d.], pp. 575–87). Despite the weighty authority of these theologians, however, the *parakīyā* doctrine eventually won out. Indeed, the *svakīyā* doctrine was never really accepted at all, as the great majority of the cult's works testify. The matter was formally and decisively settled in the eighteenth century when a debate in Bengal was arranged between advocates of the two positions. The proponents of the *parakīyā* doctrine, led by Rādhāmohana-ṭhākura, were triumphant, and the *parakīyā* doctrine was firmly established as orthodox. The dominance and eventual triumph of the *parakīyā* doctrine emphasize the revolutionary otherness of that world to which Kṛṣṇa's flute calls the *gopīs*. By answering its call they leave conventional morality behind to revel illicitly with Kṛṣṇa, their lover. For a discussion of the *parakīyā* doctrine and its place in Bengal Vaiṣṇavism, see Edward C. Dimock, *The Place of the Hidden Moon: Erotic Mysticism in the Vaiṣṇava-sahajiyā Cult of Bengal* (Chicago: University of Chicago Press, 1966), especially pp. 200–215.

[60] *Bhāgavata-purāṇa* X. 21. 12 (4:94).

[61] Ibid., X. 35. 14–15 (4:144).

of the universe upon which Viṣṇu slumbers during the long cosmic night], whirl in loving delusion, yea it penetrated deep into the very bottom of the whole creation.[62]

The sweet tune that the flute produces is sublime and powerful. It spreads like lightning in all directions. It penetrates into the creation and reaches the highest heaven known as Vaikuntha.

From the heaven known as Vaikuntha it reacts with a terrific atomic force and penetrates into all ears in the creation and enchants all.[63]

The sound of Kṛṣṇa's flute is no earthly sound. Its vibrations fill the heavens and distract even the gods from their usual activities.

Even nature cannot remain unaffected. When Kṛṣṇa plays his flute the river and reeds from which the flute grew weep tears of delight.[64] When the clouds hear his flute, they hover over him to provide shade and to shower him with cooling drops of fresh water.[65] Rivers slow down when they hear his flute and grow lotuses for him.[66] The deer in the forest, hearing his flute, stand still, ears erect, attentive and motionless.[67] The whole creation can concentrate on nothing but its sound.

When my Black One put the flute to his lips the ecstasy of the sages was disturbed. The cars of the gods stopped when they heard it and the wives of the gods became like pictures. The planets and the stars did not leave their constellation; they were tied up to the sound. Joy overflowed to hear it and the immovables of water and earth moved. The movement of the moveable and the immoveable was reversed to hear the song produced by the Venu (flute). Stones began to throw up springs and the divine singers were charmed with the sweet songs. Hearing

[62]Rūpa Gosvāmin, *Vidagdha-mādhava* I. 39; quoted in Kṛṣṇadāsa Kavirāja, *Caitanya-caritāmṛta*, Antya-līlā 1 (p. 23).

[63]Kṛṣṇadāsa Kavirāja, *Caitanya-caritāmṛta*, Madhya-līlā 21. 119 (p. 538).

[64]*Bhāgavata-purāṇa* X. 21. 12–15 (4:93).

[65]Ibid., X. 21. 16 (4:94).

[66]Ibid., X. 21. 15 (4:94).

[67]Ibid., X. 35. 4–5 (4:143).

this the birds and the beasts became still and forgot their food and did not drink milk and the birds lost patience. The trees and creepers became restless and they gave out new leaves. The trees and the leaves of which were restless, became anxious to be near (him). Those, which had the buds as the horripilation of joy began to shed tears of love. Hearing it the restless wind became tired and water of the river could not move.[68]

Even Kṛṣṇa himself is not immune to the sound of his flute. In this poem by Sūrdās, Kṛṣṇa is intoxicated—enchanted and delighted by his own irresistible call.

> The flute has done her work.
> She plunders for herself, depriving us of the
> nectar of Hari's lips.
> Nanda's son [Kṛṣṇa] is under the influence of
> her music. She has cast her spell over him.
> The living and the non-living, the moving and
> the unmoving, and even the God of Love are
> spellbound.
> She distracted all, even those not easily distracted.
> The milkmaid says that the Lord, the crown of
> the wise, has fallen into her hands.[69]

By means of his flute, Kṛṣṇa fills himself and the universe with bliss. He distracts everyone and everything from normal activity and enchants them to revel in ecstasy. His flute sends shudders of delight to the very foundations of the world. Natural laws fall away as rocks and trees respond to his call and stars wander from their courses. The sound of his flute puts an abrupt end to man's mechanical, habitual activity as well as to the predictable movements of nature. His music explodes upon the world and society insisting that all else be forgotten. It is time, it proclaims, to join his symphony of joy, to frolic in the forest, to

[68]From Sūrdās's *Sūrsāgar*, in Janardan Misra, *The Religious Poetry of Surdas* (Königsberg: University of Königsberg, 1934), pp. 107–8.

[69]Surdas, "The Poems of Surdas," poem 60.

scamper in play, to realize every dream that one has ever dreamed in his world of infinite possibility. Kṛṣṇa's flute incites the world to dance, to lose itself in superfluous rhythms. It invites man to return to that carefree, playful world of his youth. It asks nothing but surrender to its frenzied tune and enthusiastic participation in its magic world. Kṛṣṇa is the master magician, ruling over a fairyland, and his wand is his flute.

The Divine Lover

The charming, youthful god who entrances all by his beauty and seduces the creation with the sound of his flute is the hero of the love-*līlā* of Vṛndāvana, the central episode of the Kṛṣṇa cult. Other gods in the Hindu pantheon indulge in amorous diversions and erotic dalliance, but Kṛṣṇa stands supreme among the gods as the Divine Lover. As the lover of Rādhā and the *gopīs*, Kṛṣṇa expresses the delightful and complex nature of the divine-human relationship that unfolds itself in ecstatic devotion.

Kṛṣṇa's activity as a lover can be considered of two general types: in relation to Rādhā alone or to a particular *gopī* and in relation to the *gopīs* as a group. The first type is more personal and complex, involving a wide range of moods and situations. The latter type is uniformly described in the various Vaiṣṇava texts. It is riotous, festive, and rollicking.

A consistent feature of the love between Rādhā and Kṛṣṇa, and indeed of love in general, is that it takes place in a world apart, in an ideal world that shuns the ordinary world.[70] Their

[70]Although Rādhā is known quite early in Indian literature, her central position in Vaiṣṇava myth and cult came much later. She is mentioned in the Prakrit work *Gahasattasai,* attributed to Hāla and probably written before the seventh century A.D. (Surdas, "The Poems of Surdas," p. 12). But she did not become popular in Sanskrit poetry until the eleventh and twelfth centuries. (Sen's *Brajabuli Literature,* p. 485, has a list of Sanskrit plays that deal with Rādhā at about this time.) If Rādhā was known to the author of the *Bhāgavata-purāṇa,* which was written sometime around A.D. 900, he chose not to mention her, even though Kṛṣṇa's

love takes place in a magic circle where everything they see, do, and are is transformed. The entire relationship unfolds in the idyllic bowers of Vṛndāvana, away from and outside of the world of social responsibility and traditional courtship. The relationship is playful, sometimes amusing, and intimate. It is a description of the divine-human relationship as it ought to be, in the context of the Garden before the Fall. Every facet, every mood and nuance of the relationship, is cherished and doted upon by Vaiṣṇava devotees and in Vaiṣṇava texts.

The awakening of love, or the mood of first love *(pūrva-rāga)*, is prevaded by an amusing theme in which Rādhā shows a curious mixture of the girl and the woman, of curiosity and shyness. She is not yet a woman and no longer a girl. She is a flutter of girlish giggles at one moment and pensive the next. Her naïveté, girlish boldness, and womanly modesty combine to create an irresistible charm that is at once endearing and amusing. She is a favorite subject of Vaiṣṇava poets.

> The girl and the woman
> bound in one being;
> the girl puts up her hair,
> the woman lets it
> fall to cover her breasts;
> the girl reveals her arms,
> her long legs, innocently bold;
> the woman wraps her shawl modestly about her,
> her open glance a little veiled.

---

dalliance with the *gopīs* is central there. Her acceptance by the Vaiṣṇavas seems to have taken place, therefore, sometime between the composition of the *Bhāgavata-purāṇa* and Jayadeva's *Gīta-govinda*, written near the end of the twelfth century in Bengal. In this work the sole theme is the love between Rādhā and Kṛṣṇa. Nimbārka seems to have been the first well-known religious leader to regard Rādhā as central to his cult (thirteenth century). For a discussion of the origin and development of the Rādhā cult, particularly its history in Bengal, see S. C. Mukherji, *A Study of Vaiṣṇavism in Ancient and Medieval Bengal* (Calcutta: Punthi Pustak, 1966), App. A, pp. 183–95.

Restless feet, a blush on the young breasts,
hint at her heart's disquiet:
behind her closed eyes
Kāma [the god of love] awakes, born of imagination,
the god.
Vidyāpati says, Krishna, bridgroom,
be patient, she will be brought to you.[71]

Another playful theme in this early stage of love is Rādhā's coyness, both unpremeditated and strategic. A girlfriend has brought her to Kṛṣṇa, and she is about to be left alone with him for the first time.

Fingering the border of her friend's sari, nervous
and afraid,
sitting tensely on the edge of Krishna's couch,
as her friend left she too looked to go
but in desire Krishna blocked her way.
He was infatuated, she bewildered;
he was clever, and she naive.
He put out his hand to touch her; she quickly
pushed it away.
He looked into her face, her eyes filled with tears.
He held her forcefully, she trembled violently
and hid her face from his kisses behind the edge of
her sari.
Then she lay down, frightened, beautiful as a doll;
he hovered like a bee round a lotus in a painting.
Govinda-dāsa says, Because of this,
drowned in the well of her beauty,
Krishna's lust was changed.[72]

Here Rādhā's coyness is genuine. In the following poem, however, her go-between advises her to employ coyness as a strategy in the game of love:

[71]Dimock, *In Praise of Krishna,* p. 7.

[72]Ibid., p. 11.

First, you will decorate your hairs and besmear
(sandal) paste (over your body). Then you will
paint your unsteady eyes with collyrium.
You will go with all your limbs covered with cloth.
You will remain at a distance so that he may
become (very much) desirous (of meeting) you.
O damsel, first you will manifest (signs of) bashfulness,
and with your side-glances you will
arouse Cupid.
You will cover (one half of) your breasts and expose
the other half. Every moment you will make the
knot in the lower garment tighter.
You will show anger and then exhibit some love (for
him). You will preserve the sentiment so that
he may come again and again.
O damsel, what further instructions in the science of
love shall I give you?
Cupid himself will become the guide and will tell
you everything, Vidyapati says.[73]

The nature of love—or, more exactly, courtship—as a game is clear here. Coyness and mock resistance heighten the suspense about who will "win." It is a ploy by which Rādhā elicits Kṛṣṇa's feelings for her before she has actually offered herself. It is a means of forcing Kṛṣṇa to declare himself first.

The loveplay of Rādhā and Kṛṣṇa is pervaded with mock quarrels and fits of temper that surround their dalliance with a sense of frivolity. The following passage from the *Brahma-vaivarta-purāṇa* is a good example:

The expert Kriṣṇa playfully denuded Râdhâ of her dress and ornaments; and Râdhâ denuded him of his crest and apparel. As both were expert in the game, no harm accrued to any of them. Kriṣṇa took away the looking-glass of gem from her hands; and she snatched away from him his melodious flute. Râdhâ enchanted the mind of Kriṣṇa and Kriṣṇa

[73]Vidyapati, *The Songs of Vidyapati,* trans. Subhadra Jha (Banaras: Motilal Banarsidass, 1954), no. 62, p. 63.

charmed her heart. When this fight of love was over, the crooked eyed Râdhâ returned to him his flute; and Krișṇa returned to her the looking-glass and the lotus used as a toy to play with, fastened her chignon, and marked her forehead with vermillion.[74]

From time to time one or the other will have a fit of pique and feign indifference toward the other. In this poem Rādhā is speaking to Kṛṣṇa's messenger, an old woman, and scowls at the necessity of Kṛṣṇa's using a go-between:

From the time our eyes first met
our longing grew.
He was not only the desirer, I not only the
desired:
passion ground our hearts together in its mortar.
Friend, do not forget to recall to Krishna
how it was with us then.
Then we required no messenger, sought
only each other's lips for our love.
It was the god of love himself who united us,
he of the five arrows . . .
But now my lordly lover has learned new manners,
now he sends *you*, herald of his indifference!
So, with anger like a king's increasing,
sings the poet Rāmānanda Rāy.[75]

And in this poem Rādhā's pique has reached the point where in her sulking she mocks Kṛṣṇa's entreaties and sends him on his way peremptorily:

[74]*Brahma-vaivarta-purāṇa*, Kṛṣṇa Janma Khanda 15. 151–58 (2:159).

[75]Dimock, *In Praise of Krishna*, p. 41. The poet's signature line *(bhanitā)* in this poem is interesting. He has written the poem in the mood of Rādhā and shares with her his anger at Kṛṣṇa's indifference. These signature lines illustrate an important point. The poems are not simply poems but also religious offerings in which the various moods of love are created. The poems are meant to be entered into. The devotee is to imagine himself, along with the poet, as part of the action. In other words, the myth is to be realized in the devotee's imaginative life. The myth of Rādhā and Kṛṣṇa is both a paradigm for devotion and an ongoing drama in which the devotee seeks to participate vicariously or directly.

The marks of fingernails are on your breast
and my heart burns.
Kohl of someone's eyes upon your lips
darkens my face.
I am awake all night;
your eyes are red,
So why do you entreat me, Kān,
Saying that you and I have but one heart?
You come with choking voice
while I want to weep.
"Only our bodies are apart."
But mine is light,
and yours is dark.
Go home, then,
says Govinda-dāsa.[76]

The reconciliations that follow such quarrels and fits of pique frequently have a comic theme that shows the previous anger to have been false.

Having come, *Madhava* opened the door of the room in
which *Radha* was resting.
In her anger on account of drowsiness, she looked
with a suppressed smile at (him; her face)
looked as if a half of the moon had risen (above
in the sky).
Radha began to bewail and speak to *Madhava.*
Who, in youth, beauty, accomplishment or in
any other quality, is superior to me? Who
is the girl who is more accomplished than
myself?
"I delayed at *Mathura.*" Then why did you not
send a messenger?
"There I met some traders and fell asleep."
Your mind is fickle: it is not steady: you
do not assume gravity.
She cast her side-glances and with a little

[76]Ibid., p. 45.

smile (she said) your body is black even
within. Vidyapati says.[77]

In the following passage from the *Rasikapriyā*, Rādhā brings about reconciliation on her own initiative in a devious and delightful way:

Rādhā came smilingly to Kṛishṇa and sang him a tale of love. She then asked him to explain to her the meaning of some of the sequences in the story: the simultaneous partaking by the lovers of the nectar of each other's mouths, and of other parts of the body which in consequence suffered amorous injuries by nails and teeth. Enclosing him in an embrace, she also asked him, on an oath, what mode of embracing the lovers in the tale had adopted. Thus did Rādhā herself make up her quarrel with her lover today.[78]

The love affair between Rādhā and Kṛṣṇa is full of laughing and joking, which surrounds the relationship with a cheerful air. "In that charming garden by the Yamunā there blew the South breeze, and they both were joking and talking intimately, and amusing each other."[79] This lighter theme dominates their love to the almost total exclusion of the brooding, oppressive aspects of love. The bitterness of recrimination, guilt, and hurt is never allowed to color the relationship. It is as if genuine love had nothing to do with the world of nastiness and jealousy. In the magic circle things are always light and cheerful. Anger and pique are brief, serving only to heighten the bliss of reconciliation. Neither lover is ever injured permanently.

The lovers' dialogue also underlines the light, playful nature of their relationship. Kṛṣṇa especially is made to embody the model of the clever, sporting young man whose forte is humorous conversation. The dramas by Bengal Vaiṣṇavas that portray

[77]Vidyapati, *The Songs of Vidyapati*, no. 220, p.223.

[78]In M. S. Randhawa, *Kangra Paintings on Love* (New Delhi: National Museum, 1962), p. 95.

[79]Devakīnandana-dāsa, in Sen, *Brajabuli Literature*, p. 49.

Kṛṣṇa illustrate this well. While the dramas frequently resort to homilies on the superiority of *bhakti*, they take delight in portraying Kṛṣṇa as a witty hero who spends his time amusing his friends with jokes, teasing and playing tricks on the *gopīs*, and bantering with Rādhā.[80]

The playful, amusing nature of Rādhā and Kṛṣṇa's love, then, serves to underline the fact that the relationship takes place in a world apart, far removed from the harsh world of work and worrisome duty. And within the enchanted realm of their love each finds a new freedom, particularly Rādhā. Within the love relationship her deepest feelings finally can be expressed. Her longings and secret dreams are fulfilled in her intimacy with Kṛṣṇa.

> Lovely Rādhā was seated on (Kṛṣṇa's) lap. The two (lovers) were engrossed in each other's fresh youthfulness. Madly in love the Two (were) in mutual embrace, (and this looked) as if a golden creeper had entwined a *tamāla* tree. Their eyes were unsteady for the ecstasy of love. . . . Their loveliness was reflected on each other's eyes, looking at which the moon disappeared from the sky. The two golden cups (*i.e.* Rādhā's breasts) were covered up by the hands (of Kṛṣṇa). Laughing they talked of their secret feelings.[81]

In the following poem by Vidyāpati, the bondage of love is called a net, but within that net Rādhā finds her freedom:

> As I near the bed,
> He smiles and gazes.
> Flower-arrows fill the world.
> The sport of love,
> Its glow and luxuries
> Are indescribable, O friend,
> And when I yield myself,
> His joy is endless.

[80] Jīva Gosvāmin's *Gopāla-campū* and Rūpa Gosvāmin's *Dāna-keli-kaumudī* are typical of this genre of literature.

[81] Vāsudeva-dāsa, in Sen, *Brajabuli Literature*, pp. 365–66.

Freeing my skirt,
He snatches at my garland.
My downcast mind
Is freed of frontiers,
Though my life is held
In the net of his love.
He drinks my lips.
With heart so thrilled,
He takes my clothes away.
I lose my body
At his touch
And long to check
But grant his love.
Says Vidyāpati:
Sweet as honey
Is the talk of a girl in love.[82]

The flood of emotions that overcomes the lovers, whether in the presence of the beloved or not, is a popular theme in Vaiṣṇava literature. The poets delight in depicting Rādhā's distracted frame of mind, her rapidly changing moods, or her hopelessly obvious behavior that is meant to be discreet. In the *Rasikapriyā*, under a discussion of external indications of love, Keśav Dās speaks of *vibhrama-bhāva,* or flutter. As an example of this, he describes Rādhā when she hears Kṛṣṇa's flute. She puts her necklace around her waist, her earrings on her hands, and generally loses control of her senses. And when Kṛṣṇa sees Rādhā he drops the betel in his hands and inadvertently begins to chew on a lotus.[83] The height of emotion is reached when the lovers, totally immersed in each other, consummate their love in the bowers of Vṛndāvana. Shame is completely forgotten, and they behave with abandon, frenzied and intoxicated. In this state they are completely enclosed in their own special world. They are free to behave in any way they choose. In the following

[82]Vidyāpati, *Love Songs of Vidyāpati.* no. 68, p.107.

[83]Randhawa, *Kangra Paintings on Love*, p. 56.

poem, Rādhā loses all inhibitions and takes the dominant part in the lovemaking:

> Her massive locks are dishevelled. She is the goddess of amorous sport, embodied and incarnate. Their passionate love is excessive. So the girl behaves as a man. . . . Her vase-shaped breasts are turned upside down, as if the god of love is pouring out the nectar of love. Over them the hands of the dearest (lover) have been placed, as if (a pair of) *cakravākas* are sitting over (a pair of) lotuses. Bangles and bells at her girdle are jingling, as if the band of joy has been struck by the company of the god of love.[84]

In the next poem the sight of Kṛṣṇa is sufficient for Rādhā to lose all her modesty. And everywhere she sees nothing but Kṛṣṇa, so immersed in him is she.

> After seeing him the eyes fled off (the face):
> it seemed as if the lotus, having discarded
> the sun was running away.
> The moon and the lily met each other. I could
> hide the expression of love with a trick.
> O lady, I saw *Madhava* today. Having forsaken
> its gravity my bashfulness vanished away.
> The knot in the lower garment became loose and
> fell on the ground. I was hiding my body
> under my body.
> Even my own heart seemed to be of another person.
> In all directions I saw Kṛṣṇa and Kṛṣṇa alone.
> Vidyapati says.[85]

The lovers in this condition are so absorbed in each other that they can barely cope with normal life. The following is a description of Rādhā's distracted and absentminded frame of mind, from the *Rasikapriyā*:

[84]Kavirañjana (Vidyāpati ii), in Sen, *Brajabuli Literature*, pp. 145–46.

[85]Vidyapati, *The Songs of Vidyapati*, no. 66, p. 67.

She stares as if startled; her heart beats heavily and seeing her own shadow she loses herself in thought. Her answers are irrelevant to the questions asked of her; in separation she has become an altogether changed person. . . . Thus deranged, she is now indifferent to her veil, her garments and her ornaments.[86]

Here Kṛṣṇa's state of mind is described, and it is clear that he is as obviously affected as Rādhā—that the divine is also hopelessly and helplessly entangled in the divine-human love affair. One of Rādhā's friends is speaking to her shortly after having seen Kṛṣṇa:

With tearful eyes and dazed mind he gazes all around, then stares fixedly, and then walks away hurriedly. He keeps brooding with agitated mind and fever in his body. Sometimes he weeps and sometimes laughs. Fear-stricken and agitated in my mind, I have come to tell you of his condition. He is talking so incoherently that I fear lest the secret of his love for you may not be disclosed.[87]

Finally, the realm of Rādhā and Kṛṣṇa's love dalliance is a world of joy. Their love is a celebration that enables Rādhā to enter completely that extraordinary, other world of the divine where everything is resolved in bliss. Rādhā sings:

The moon has shone upon me,
the face of my beloved.
O night of joy!

Joy permeates all things.
My life: joy,
my youth: fulfillment.

Today my house is again
home,
today my body is
my body.

[86]From Keśav Das, *Rasikapriyā,* in Randhawa, *Kangra Paitings on Love* p. 112.

[87]Ibid., p. 117.

The god
of destiny smiled on me.
No more doubt.
Let the nightingales sing, then,
let there be myriad
rising moons, let Kāma's
five arrows become five thousand
and the south wind
softly, softly, blow;
for now my body has meaning
in the presence of my beloved.
Vidyāpati says, Your luck is great:
may this return of love be blessed.[88]

The joy of the loving couple is also the joy of the *gopīs* of Vṛndāvana. Turning to the second type of Kṛṣṇa's amorous dalliance, we find the emphasis is on Kṛṣṇa as the ringmaster of a festival of love. He instigates it, leads it, enjoys it, and is by far the most accomplished at it. By means of his flute he beckons the women of Vṛndāvana to that separate world of his where intoxication and abandon, joy and rollicking sport reign supreme. The *Brahma-vaivarta-purāṇa* takes special delight in describing Kṛṣṇa's sports with hundreds of *gopīs* in the forest of Vṛndāvana.

Some of the cow herdesses . . . out of fun forcibly took away the flute from the hands of Lord Krisṇa. Then they pulled his yellow dress. Some passionate girl denuded him of his clothes, took away his yellow garment and then in jest returned it to him. . . . Some cowherdess intentionally showed to him her smiling lunar face full of glances, rising breast and delicate waist. . . . Some pulled his crest and attached to it the plumage of peacock. Others adorned the crest with wreaths of flowers, other fanned and tended the lord of their lives with white chowries. . . . Some danced and sang with Krisṇa in the centre; others forcibly caused him to dance. Krisṇa also out of fun, dragged the clothes of some milk-maid, made her naked and then returned the clothes to her.[89]

[88]Dimock, *In Praise of Krishna*, p. 66.

[89]*Brahma-vaivarta-purāṇa*, Kṛṣṇa Janma Khaṇḍa 28. 84–93 (2:232).

The text goes on to describe an increasingly tumultuous scene in which the clothes of the *gopīs* fall off in their excitement. Kṛṣṇa, surrounded by his band of impassioned women, caresses and makes love to them all. When their love celebration was in full swing even the gods assembled to watch.[90] The *Govinda-līlāmṛta* is as explicit as the *Brahma-vaivarta-purāṇa* in describing Kṛṣṇa's erotic dalliance with the *gopīs*.

Kṛṣṇa was dancing. He paused and admired the girls. He kissed some of them on the cheeks and lips, looked at others with desire, and fondled the breasts of others, marking them with his nails. In that game of *rāsa* he had sexual intercourse with Rādhā and others, and thus had intercourse with himself.[91]

The last phrase of this passage suggests a peculiar Bengal Vaiṣṇava doctrine that declares the *gopīs* to be Kṛṣṇa's own *śaktis* (dynamic manifestations). In dalliance with them he is, therefore, taking delight in himself. Another passage from the *Govinda-līlāmṛta* hints at the same thing by comparing Kṛṣṇa's sport with the *gopīs* to a boy playing with his own image in a mirror:

Kṛṣṇa in this way made his own wives, the fair ladies of Vrāja, sing and dance, and they also made him dance and sing, which he did wonderfully. He praised them, and they praised him. He played just like a boy playing with his own reflection.[92]

The boisterous frolic of Kṛṣṇa and the *gopīs* continues in the waters of the Jumna and suggests the atmosphere of a carnival.

Krisṇa . . . sprinkled Râdhâ's body with water. Râdhâ also poured . . . water on the body of the passionate Krisṇa. Hari snatched away the cloth of Râdhâ. . . . Then he tore her wreath and loosened

[90]Ibid., 22. 107–13 (2:232–33).

[91]Kṛṣṇadāsa Kavirāja, *Govinda-līlāmṛta*, p. 1281.

[92]Ibid.

her chignon. . . . Then Krisṇa after having displayed the abashed, naked Râdhâ to the cowherdesses threw her again at a distance into the water. Râdhâ got up in haste from the water, seized Krisṇa by force, took away his flute in anger, cast it at a distance, snatched his yellow garment, tore the wreath of wild flowers and sprinkled water on him again and again. . . . In this way the imaginary forms of the Lord merrily played with the cowherdesses on the coasts of the Yamunâ and within the water. After the play was over, the naked Lord and Râdhâ both came to the coast and demanded their clothes from one another.[93]

As a male elephant in rut, after sporting with female elephants, goes to a river for rest, so Kṛṣṇa too, after dancing excessively with the *gopīs*, . . . began to sport in the waters of the Jumna. Drawing the tired *gopīs* by the hand, he plunged into the water and began to sport there. Sometimes with one, sometimes with five or six at a time, and sometimes with all the *gopīs*, Kṛṣṇa, in separate groups (being omnipresent), began mock fights in the water.[94]

In the atmosphere of the carnival, normal laws, moral as well as civil, are suspended. It is a time when behavior can be spontaneous and without regret. The carnival is an anarchical celebration where the normal world has no place. And this is the world of Kṛṣṇa. His world is a sporting ground where nothing is done out of necessity or by custom. There all activity is free and indulgent.

The great intoxicator himself, finally, also becomes intoxicated by drinking wine and indulging his passion. In the divine-human relationship God shows himself to be as frenzied, as passionate, and as carried away as man.

By means of his divine power Kṛṣṇa stood between each pair of women [by multiplying himself]. Joking and laughing with them he kissed and bit their lips and gave them fruit mixed with honey. . . . Then he became intoxicated with *kandarpa* [a kind of wine, also the name of the god of love and sexual passion] and *madya* wine. He took Rādhā

[93]*Brahma-vaivarta-purāṇa*, Kṛṣṇa Janma Khaṇḍa 28. 128–41 (2:233–34).

[94]Kṛṣṇadāsa Kavirāja, *Govinda-līlāmṛta*, pp. 1294–95.

into a bower by the riverbank, and she too flared up under the same intoxicating drinks.[95]

The intimate and playful themes that run through Kṛṣṇa's love for Rādhā and the festival nature of his dalliance with the *gopīs* portray a vision of the divine that is approachable, warm, irresistible, blissful, and intoxicating. Kṛṣṇa moves in a realm of love and lovemaking that invites (indeed, demands) a total, impassioned response. All those who enter this realm are freed from bondage to the ordinary and customary, freed to behave imaginatively and spontaneously. The erotic aspect of this other world is not degrading but life-affirming. Erotic dalliance shuns the world of taboos and lives for the moment. It is an ovation to all that is vigorous and full of joy. The young god Kṛṣṇa is an unrepentant reveler stirring all those who join with him to uncontrollable frenzy. In the world of the great lover Kṛṣṇa, the *gopīs*, as representatives of the human, expand themselves; they plumb depths and reach heights of emotion that are impossible within the humdrum world of habitual action. They leave behind the ordinary and participate in the extraordinary. Under the influence of the intoxicating and intoxicated god they lose their inhibitions and revel in playful freedom.

[95]Ibid., p. 1288.

CHAPTER II

Introduction

The essential revelations seen in the vision of the cowherd Kṛṣṇa should be clear from the preceding descriptions of his life in Vṛndāvana. The cowherd youth reveals the divine as free and spontaneous, rambunctious and anarchical. He also reveals it as exquisitely beautiful and graceful, attracting all who sense his presence. And he reveals it as a presence that incites man to frenzy, abandon, and passionate involvement. The divine as embodied in Kṛṣṇa the cowherd youth beckons man to leave the world of the humdrum and ordinary, to join him in an "other" world of incomparable bounty, beauty, and ecstasy. He reveals the divine as eminently approachable, a presence to be intimately enjoyed in love rather than adored in humility.

The myth of the tumultuous cowherd Kṛṣṇa also portrays a vision of the divine that goes against the stereotype of Indian spirituality as quietistic, meditative, and still. It might be tempting to consider Kṛṣṇa an aberration or deviation from the central vision of the Hindu tradition. The great popularity of the dark god, however, is enough to cause some hesitation before labeling his myth or cult an aberration. Given the fact that Kṛṣṇa is perhaps the most popular of all Hindu deities, it is apparent that in some ways he epitomizes, or expresses, central truths of the Hindu tradition.

The following discussion attempts to show how Kṛṣṇa articulates and dramatically expresses some central themes of the Hindu tradition. The themes are not chosen at random but are purposely selected for their importance to the tradition. They are *bhakti* (devotion), *ānanda* (bliss), and *līlā* (play).

The Kṛṣṇa myth illustrates other Hindu themes as well, but a discussion of these three themes should suffice to show to what extent the vision underlying the Kṛṣṇa myth is grounded in the Hindu spiritual view of things. Kṛṣṇa devotees, in their ardent adoration of the lovely god, declare their lord's transcendent uniqueness by insisting that he is the supreme expression of deity, the One from whom all other divine beings proceed. Rapt in his beauty and bewitched by his flute, they would call our attention to his absolute uniqueness. The following discussion does not deny that Kṛṣṇa is a unique, supernal expression of the divine; certainly he presents the tradition with a uniquely beautiful vision of the divine. This discussion simply tries to illustrate another truth: that Kṛṣṇa is also a Hindu deity and as such expresses truths of that larger tradition.

BHAKTI: FROM LORD TO LOVER

Throughout his history Kṛṣṇa has been inextricably bound up with Hindu devotion. In the *Bhagavadgītā* (and elsewhere in the *Mahābhārata*) Kṛṣṇa reveals his divine identity to Arjuna and teaches him the path of *bhakti-yoga*, the path of devotion to God. Along with the paths of knowledge *(jñāna-mārga)* and disinterested works *(karma-yoga)*, devotion *(bhakti)* is presented as a means to salvation and even as an end in itself. Whether the path of *bhakti* is the highest path offered in the *Gītā* is a debatable point. It is certainly clear enough, however, that *bhakti* is central to the *Gītā* and that it is Kṛṣṇa who reveals this path and reveals himself as the object of devotion. Within the context of his role in the epic as a counselor, friend, and charioteer, then, Kṛṣṇa emerges as the supreme object of devotion in this famous text, and it is within the context of devotion that Kṛṣṇa's subsequent history must be understood. It is not an exaggeration to say that Kṛṣṇa's history is by and large the history of Hindu devotionalism. His mythology, iconography, and cult wax and wane and are modified in consonance with the changing nature of the *bhakti* cults. Or perhaps it would be more accurate to say that the devotional cults develop and modify in response to the ongoing revelation of the Lord Kṛṣṇa.

The nature of devotion in the *Bhagavadgītā*, particularly in contrast to subsequent developments, is generally staid and pietistic. Discipline and sacrifice are the guidelines that channel devotion. There is little spontaneity on the part of the devotee. Indeed, in some passages it is suggested that *bhakti* may be employed as a means to an end, as a means to yoking the mind in the performance of disciplined action (9. 27–28). Nor is intimacy the context of devotion in the *Gītā*. The attitude of the devotee, typified by Arjuna, is one of subservience. This is strikingly clear when Kṛṣṇa reveals his cosmic form. Arjuna is struck with wonder and bows down before him in awe.

> Making a reverent gesture, trembling, the
> Diademed (Arjuna)
> Made obeisance and spoke yet again to Kṛṣṇa,
> Stammering, greatly affrighted, bowing down.[1]

Arjuna is so frightened that he asks Kṛṣṇa to reassume his former appearance as his charioteer.

> Having seen what was never seen before, I am thrilled,
> And (at the same time) my heart is shaken with fear;
> Show me, O God, that same form of Thine (as before)!
> Be merciful, Lord of Gods, Abode of the World![2]

In the *Bhagavadgītā* the divine-human relationship is that between a lord and his servant. The great warrior hero, Arjuna, cannot withstand the direct vision of the divine. He trembles and is reduced to dust and ashes before the majesty of God. The terrible, awesome nature of the divine completely dominates

[1]*Bhagavadgītā* 11. 35; *The Bhagavad Gītā*, trans. Franklin Edgerton (New York: Harper & Row, 1964), p. 58.

[2]Ibid., 11. 45 (p. 60).

the relationship. There is only one attitude appropriate to man before the divine, and that is humility.

By the time of the *Bhāgavata-purāṇa* (tenth century A.D.), and perhaps as early as the *Harivaṁśa* and the *Viṣṇu-purāṇa* (circa A.D. 400), Hindu devotional cults had undergone some important changes. Particularly in South India, between the seventh and tenth centuries A.D., devotion began to take on a fervent, impassioned quality. In the poetry of the Tamil Śaivite Nāyanārs, devotion is expressed, not in terms of trembling and awe (although these are not entirely lacking), but in terms of ecstatic love.

> Into my vile body of flesh
> you came, as though it were a temple of gold,
> and soothed me wholly and saved me,
> O Lord of Grace, O Gem Most pure.
> Sorrow and birth and death and illusion
> you took from me, and set me free.
> O bliss! O Light! I have taken refuge in you,
> and never can I be parted from you.[3]

It was in the South, too, that *bhakti* took on many of its characteristically "protestant" features. The Tamil saints came from all castes, and several rejected outright "the religion of the priest, ritual, and book," constantly rebelling against such "establishment" virtues as wealth and caste *dharma*.[4] In the South the tendency reached its culmination in the devotional poetry of the Liṅgāyata *sampradāya*, a Śaivite devotional cult originating in the twelfth century in the Kannada area. Its founder, Basava, ridiculed the formal, ritual aspects of brāhmanic religion by declaring that devotion to Śiva alone is all that matters in man's spiritual quest. This devotion and this quest are all-consuming

[3]Māṇikka Vāchakar, in A. L. Basham, *The Wonder That Was India* (New York: Grove Press, 1954), p. 331.

[4]A. K. Ramanujan, "Medieval 'Protestant' Movements" (lecture, Introduction to Indian Civilization, University of Chicago, February 7, 1966).

and have little or nothing to do with traditional Hindu *dharma*. A few Liṅgāyata poems will make clear the new emphases in these South Indian *bhakti* cults.

They plunge
Wherever they see water.
They circumambulate
every tree they see.
How can they know you
O Lord
who adore
waters that run dry
trees that wither?[5]

The pot is a god. The winnowing
fan is a god. The stone in the
street is a god. The comb is a
god. The bowstring is also a
god. The bushel is a god and the
spouted cup is a god.
Gods, gods, there are so many
there's no place left
for a foot.
There is only
one god. He is our Lord
of the Meeting Rivers.[6]

Even traditional good works are shunned in the poems of these saints. True devotion, according to Allāma, has nothing at all to do with social virtues. While carrying out one's social *dharma* is not necessarily condemned, one feels that it is strictly beside the point.

[5]Basava (twelfth-century founder of the Liṅgāyata *sampradāya*), in A. K. Ramanujan, trans., *Speaking of Śiva* (Baltimore: Penguin Books, 1973), no. 581, p. 85. Basava's poems have also been translated into English in the *Vacanas of Basavaṇṇa*, ed. H. Deveerappa, trans. L. M. A. Menezes and S. M. Angadi (Sirigere, Mysore: Annana Balaga, 1967), where the above poem is no. 579, p. 189.

[6]Basava, in Ramanujan, trans., *Speaking of Śiva*, no. 563, p. 84; *Vacanas*, no. 561, p. 182.

Feed the poor
tell the truth
make water-places
for the thirsty
and build tanks for a town—
you may then go to heaven
after death, but you'll get nowhere
near the truth of Our Lord.[7]

These poems typify the tenor of the *bhakti* movement in the South and suggest the mood that the *bhakti* movements of the North were to assume. Vis-à-vis the type of *bhakti* that is revealed in the *Bhagavadgītā*, there are two important changes that have come about. Intense emotion and often abandon are central elements in the poems.[8] Compared to these South Indian saints, the *bhakti* of the *Gītā* seems a bit staid and passionless. In part, perhaps, this intense emotion follows from the nature of the god who is worshiped. In the *Gītā*, Viṣṇu was revealed in all his majesty and caused Arjuna to tremble before him. In the poems of the Aḷvārs and the Kannada Śaivite saints, God is primarily a person, often a lover. The relationship is not necessarily between equals, but it is far more intimate than the *bhakti* of the *Gītā* The second important change is the devotee's relationship or attitude toward society. The Kannada saints often show contempt for established religion and tradition. *Bhakti* for them has nothing to do with habit or custom. It takes place outside the status quo, and in some cases we are told that the true devotee cannot serve God and society at the same time. The *Gītā* taught man to live in society but to maintain an attitude of disinterestedness. For the new *bhakti* the possibility of man living in but not of the world is brought into question and at times is rejected outright.

[7]Allāma, in Ramanujan, trans., *Speaking of Śiva*, no. 959, p. 167.

[8]It is interesting to note that the *Bhāgavata-purāṇa* is also of southern origin and quite explicitly teaches a frenzied kind of devotion. See Kṛṣṇa's discourse with Uddhava, especially XI. 14. 23–24.

The story of Kṛṣṇa the cowherd, particularly his passionate affair with the *gopīs* and Rādhā, is an appropriate and beautiful vehicle for expressing the new, impassioned, all-consuming type of devotion. The story of the young god, particularly as it is told in the *Bhāgavata-purāṇa* (a work of South India), presents us with a divine being and a cast of characters in a dramatic context that picks up and epitomizes almost every earlier theme of the previous southern cults.

The drama, in the first place, takes place outside the normal confines of society. It occurs in a humble cowherd village or in the forests of Vṛndāvana. Indeed, the whole affair *is* out of this world. There is very little reference throughout Kṛṣṇa's sojourn in Vṛndāvana to traditional Hindu society. Vṛndāvana is a charmed place, idyllic, free, and without the strictures of ordinary life. It is only after Kṛṣṇa has left Vṛndāvana that he begins to assume social responsibilities, and it is only in Vṛndāvana that he is adored in the subsequent Kṛṣṇa cults. True devotion is a mad, intoxicating affair that needs such a setting to express itself fully. The normal world is inhibiting, full of obstacles and distractions. In the bowers of Vṛndāvana the devotee can involve himself completely. The Kṛṣṇa cults do not condemn society, nor do they condemn the religion of the priest, ritual, and book. But they do not praise society or established religion, and it is clear that they long for the freedom of idyllic Vṛndāvana, where they can dote on their Lord totally.

The cowherd women as the heroines of this drama further underline the nature of this type of devotion. They are ideal representatives of a devotional life that emphasizes spontaneity, passion, and an uninhibited response to the lovely blue god. While such legendary devotees as Nārada and Prahlāda are still important devotional models in the *Bhāgavata-purāṇa*, the *gopīs* are low-caste, ignorant peasant women. They are not known for their religious austerity or for their ethical and social virtue. They are devotees par excellence precisely because they turn their backs on society and their responsibilities to answer the call of Kṛṣṇa's flute. They are paradigmatic because of their intense passion for Kṛṣṇa, because they ignore all barriers in order to be with him alone. In contrast to the *gopīs*, the *Bhāgavata-purāṇa* portrays the *brāhmans* as stubborn and willful, refusing to recognize Kṛṣṇa as Lord of the universe.[9] The fact that the *gopīs* are superior to the *brāhmans* underlines that *bhakti* is considered superior to any other religious path and that this path may be followed outside, or even with a certain disdain for, society.

In imitating the *gopīs* one transcends society and traditional religion. "He who aspires to the feeling of the Gopis, renounces everything of the Vedic religion. For he works only for loving faith in the Lord Krishna."[10] When one's "greed" for Kṛṣṇa reaches a certain point (when it approximates that of the *gopīs*), the injunctions of the *Śāstras* and *Vedas* become irrelevant.[11] In Gauḍīya (or Bengal) Vaiṣṇavism the devotee consciously imitates the *gopīs*[12] by devoting his whole mind and being to becoming a *gopī* in an attempt to transcend the phenomenal world of custom and tradition. The passionate affair between man

[9] *Bhāgavata-purāṇa* X. 23 (4: 99–104). The *brāhmans'* wives, however, do respond affirmatively to Kṛṣṇa. The *Purāṇa* generally regards orthodox religion as useless and the *brāhmans* as stubborn. For a discussion of the social attitudes of the *Bhāgavata-purāṇa*, see Thomas J. Hopkins, "The Social Teachings of the *Bhāgavata Purāṇa*," in Milton Singer, ed., *Krishna: Myths, Rites, and Attitudes* (Honolulu: East-West Center Press, 1966), pp. 3–22.

[10] Kṛṣṇadāsa Kavirāja, *Caitanya-caritāmṛta*, Madhya-līlā 8. 177 (p. 171).

[11] Ibid., 22. 31 (p. 549).

[12] The technical term for such imitation is *rāgānugā* in Bengal Vaiṣṇavism. The details of this devotional technique are described in Rūpa Gosvāmin's *Bhakti-rasāmṛta-sindhuh*, vol. 1, trans. Tridaṇḍi Swāmī Bhakti Hṛdaya Bon Mahārāj (Vrindaban: Institute of Oriental Philosophy, 1965). De's *Vaisnava Faith and Movement*, pp. 176–80, also discusses *rāgānugā* in some detail. The Bengal Vaiṣṇavas, although stressing the importance of becoming a *gopī* in one's devotional life, do not encourage imitating the *gopīs* in external appearance or socially illicit behavior. The technique is strictly mental and emotional.

and Kṛṣṇa is subject to no law. It is a spontaneous affair, an affair that transcends tradition and morality.[13]

In the *bhakti* cults the devotional fact is clear: *bhakti* is the preeminent path to salvation, the path that is most pleasing to God as well as most satisfying and natural to man. In *bhakti* theology this truth is substantiated by the conviction that *bhakti* is man's *svadharma*, his essential duty.[14] Through *bhakti* alone does man realize his true *dharma*.

> It is assumed that, when the spirit is freed from all such extraneous impurities, the natural condition of the spirit is its natural *dharma*. This *dharma* is therefore not a thing that is to be attained or achieved as an external acquirement, but it is man's own nature, which manifests itself as soon as the impurities are removed. . . . as soon as the extraneous elements are wiped out, the spirit shows itself in its own true nature, and then its relation to absolute truth and absolute good is self-evident.[15]

In Bengal Vaiṣṇava philosophy, *jīvas* (souls, spiritual essences) are understood to be manifestations of God's *hlādinī-śakti*, his most essential self, which is nothing but pure bliss and is epitomized by Rādhā. *Jīvas*, however, are inhibited from expressing their true nature due to the influence of *māyā*, which often makes *jīvas* averse to God. Salvation is simply the process whereby man recognizes his true nature and gives it vent in devotion to Kṛṣṇa.[16] *Bhakti* is thus not a means to an end but an

[13]"Like a covetous thief, the *Prema-bhakta* (the devotee who approaches Kṛṣṇa in the mood of selfless, passionate devotion as typified by Rādhā) loses all powers of distinguishing between good and evil" (Rūpa Gosvāmin, *Bhakti-rasāmṛta-sindhuh*, translator's Introduction, 1:xxviii).

[14]The term *svadharma* is sometimes used to refer to one's inherited, social *dharma*. I am using the term here, however, to distinguish between man's inherited duty *(dharma)* and his inherent duty *(svadharma)*.

[15]Surendranath Dasgupta, *A History of Indian Philosophy*, vol. 4: *Indian Pluralism* (London: Cambridge University Press, 1966), pp. 10–11.

[16]De, *Vaisnava Faith and Movement*, p. 355.

end in itself. The four aims of life—*kāma, artha, dharma,* and *mokṣa*—are simply forgotten when man realizes his true nature. When man expresses himself in devotion to Kṛṣṇa, when he sports with Kṛṣṇa in ecstatic bliss, all desires are fulfilled. Man becomes rapt in the intoxicating beauty of Kṛṣṇa. The *gopīs* beautifully and particularly convey what man is like when he expresses his essential nature; indeed the essential nature of all men *is* that of a *gopī*. "In truth every finite being is essentially an emanation or phase of Radha, to wit, a *mañjari* or a milkmaid of Eternal Vrindabana in the prime of perennial youth."[17]

From the *Bhagavadgītā* to the *Bhāgavata-purāṇa*, the nature of *bhakti* undergoes important changes. But the object of devotion in both is Kṛṣṇa. In consonance with the changes in the tradition, Kṛṣṇa himself changes and, in so changing, elicits a new kind of devotion and brings forward new models for devotion. On the battlefield of Kurukṣetra, standing at his post as Arjuna's faithful charioteer, Kṛṣṇa teaches an ordered, pietistic, self-conscious, controlled devotion within the framework of fulfilling one's social duty. And when he reveals his cosmic form, Arjuna's response is fear and trembling. Devotion is not an intimate, passionate affair but a disciplined concentrating of mind upon a god who reveals himself to transcend and awe man. In the *Bhāgavata-purāṇa* (and even before) devotion is intimate, passionate, intense, and topsy-turvy. The context of devotion has moved from the battlefield to the isolated glades of Vṛndāvana. The devotional paradigm is no longer a strong-willed, heroic warrior who trembles with fear before the divine, but lowly *gopī* women who do not hesitate to rush off to the forest to revel with their god. And, finally, the god himself has changed from a noble, cunning charioteer and politician to an irresistible, beautiful cowherd youth who plays a flute that intoxicates all of creation.

[17]Krishnadas, *Krishna of Vrindabana*, p. 446.

The Flute: Kṛṣṇa's Carnival of Joy

Ānanda: The Inherent Bliss of the Divine

In a well-known formula, the Absolute in Hinduism is defined as *saccidānanda:* being *(sat)*, consciousness *(cit)*, and bliss *(ānanda)*. The vision of the cowherd Kṛṣṇa is an unambiguous and dramatic illustration of the divine as essentially blissful. His irresistible and intoxicating beauty, his bewitching presence, and his melodious flute fill Vṛndāvana with joy and tumultuous celebration. His bounteous being overflows itself to dizzy the entire creation. No person or thing is immune to his flute, which calls the world to revel in ecstasy. As a manifestation of the divine, as the divine itself, the lovely black youth embodies and epitomizes the immemorial truth, affirmed in the Hindu tradition since the time of the *Upaniṣads*, that the divine in its transcendence is utterly and essentially blissful.

To appreciate fully the extent to which Kṛṣṇa expresses the nature of the divine as *ānanda*, and the extent to which Vaiṣṇavas have insisted on this truth, it is important to note a few central Vaiṣṇava theological doctrines and presuppositions.[18] These presuppositions or doctrines serve to underline what is already a devotional fait accompli: they insist upon declaring unambiguously that the cowherd youth is the most perfect manifestation of the divine and as such expresses most fully the essential nature *(svabhāva)* of the divine, which is bliss.

The first doctrine is that Kṛṣṇa is not an *avatāra* (incarnation or "descent") of the divine but the Absolute God, the *avatārin*,

[18]When using the term "Vaiṣṇava theology," I am referring primarily to the systems of North India, beginning with Nimbārka and including Vallabhācārya and the six Gosvāmins of Vṛndāvana. The Gosvāmins were scholar-devotees of Caitanya, the sixteenth-century Bengali religious saint who "reformed" Vaiṣṇavism in Bengal. Caitanya sent the six Gosvāmins to Vṛndāvana to codify the philosophy of the cult. The six are: Raghunātha-dāsa, Raghunātha Bhaṭṭa, Gopāla Bhaṭṭa, Sanātana Gosvāmin, Rūpa Gosvāmin, and Jīva Gosvāmin.

the source of all *avatāras.*[19] Just when this change in status took place is not certain, but by the time of Vallabhācārya and Caitanya (sixteenth century) it was clearly the devotional, if not the theological, fact. In the *Brahma-vaivarta-purāṇa,* of uncertain but probably recent authorship, Kṛṣṇa's supreme place is unambiguously established. In a wink of his eye, Brahmā falls, and the universes dissolve,[20] while Mahā-Viṣṇu, who holds a universe in every pore of his skin, is equal to only one-sixteenth of Kṛṣṇa.[21] In Rūpa Gosvāmin's, *Laghu-bhāgavatāmṛta* and Jīva Gosvāmin's *Śrīkṛṣṇa-saṁdarbha*, two fundamental philosophical works of the Bengal Vaiṣṇavas written during the sixteenth century, this doctrine is stated unequivocally.[22] Kṛṣṇa's biography, then, is not to be understood as that of an *avatāra* who comes to rescue the world from *adharma* (the tyranny of Kaṁsa). Rather, it is to be understood as the complete and essential manifestation of what is usually unmanifest, the revelation of the Absolute in his essential and complete form.

In both the Bengal and Vallabha schools a second teaching, or presupposition, of Vaiṣṇava theology that underlines Kṛṣṇa as the ultimate expression of divine bliss is the centrality of the *Bhāgavata-purāna,* particularly the tenth book, in which the

[19]This is obviously not the case in the *Harivaṁśa* or the *Viṣṇu-purāṇa*, where Kṛṣṇa is called "a part of a part of the supreme" (V. 1 [p. 395]). Nor is it absolutely clear in the *Bhāgavata-purāṇa*. There Kṛṣṇa is listed as the nineteenth *avatāra* of Viṣṇu (I. 3. 23 [1:10]), and his incarnation occurs in the context of rescuing the world from the tyranny of Kaṁsa. The *Purāṇa* does say, however, that "the incarnation of Sri-Krishna is identical with the Lord Himself" (I. 3. 28 [1:11]), which somewhat muddies the issue.

[20]*Brahma-vaivarta-purāṇa,* Prakṛti Khaṇḍa 7. 77 (1:107).

[21]Ibid., Kṛṣṇa Janma Khaṇḍa 5. 110 (2:117).

[22]Rūpa Gosvāmin, *Laghu-bhāgavatāmṛta*, ed. Śri Balai Cand Gosvāmin, translated into Bengali by Śrī Pran Gopan Gosvāmin (Calcutta: Śrī Śrī Mahāprabhu Mandir, 1304 B.S. [1897]), pp. 66, 73; Jīvā Gosvāmin, *Śrīkṛṣṇa-saṁdarbha.*, translated into Bengali by Śrī Pran Gopan Gosvāmin (Navadvīp: Rajani Kanta Nāth, 1332 B.S. [1925]), throughout, but especially pp. 44–47, 61–66, 71.

story of Kṛṣṇa is told. In Bengal Vaiṣṇavism there is no higher philosophical authority, and the *Bhāgavata-purāṇa* is held to be the essence of the *Upaniṣads* and *Vedas*. S. K. De says of its place: "The Bengal school . . . proceeds almost entirely on an explication of the *Bhāgavata Purāṇa*."[23] Basing itself on this scripture, then, Vaiṣṇava theology affirms that the highest God, the Absolute, is revealed as a cowherd boy who sports with cowherd boys and girls in the sylvan setting of Vṛndāvana.

Another Vaiṣṇava teaching follows from this: the eternality of Vṛndāvana. Kṛṣṇa's sport in Vṛndāvana is not held to have happened simply once upon a time. His life as set forth in the *Bhāgavata-purāṇa*, in particular his sojourn in Vṛndāvana, is a description of both an earthly manifestation *and* the eternal movement within the essence of the Godhead.[24] In Bengal Vaiṣṇava theology a distinction is made between Kṛṣṇa's manifest *(prakaṭa)* and unmanifest *(aprakaṭa) līlās* (literally "playings").[25] According to this teaching, Kṛṣṇa's earthly sport in Vṛndāvana is simply a making manifest of what is ordinarily unmanifest. Or, to put it the other way, Gokula (the name of Vṛndāvana and its surrounding area) has been translated into Goloka (Kṛṣṇa's eternal realm, even above Viṣṇu's heaven, Vaikuṇṭha).

By the Bhagavat's inscrutable power *(acintya-prabhāva)*, therefore, his highest Paradise, which is situated beyond all the Lokas [divine domains], also exists on the phenomenal earth. The terrestrial Goloka or Vṛndāvana is thus not essentially different but really identical with the celestial Goloka or Vṛndāvana, and the Lord Kṛṣṇa exists eternally in both places with the same retinue.[26]

[23]De, *Vaisnava Faith and Movement*, p. 227.

[24]S. K. De, *Bengal's Contribution to Sanskrit Literature and Studies in Bengal Vaisnavism* (Calcutta: Firma K. L. Mukhopadhyay, 1960), p.114.

[25]For a discussion of this, see Rādhāgovinda Nāth, *Srī Srī Caitanya-caritāmṛta Bhumika* (Bengali) (Calcutta: published by Jatīndra Bimat Caudhurī at Śrī Guru Library, 1958), pp. 200–201.

[26]De, *Vaisnava Faith and Movement*, p. 334.

Kṛṣṇa's childhood, adolescence, and love for Rādhā and the *gopīs* are forever taking place in the paradise of Goloka. Each aspect of his biography, every incident, is therefore eternal.[27] Within the Godhead, in the highest heaven, the divine sports in ecstasy constantly, and this sport is identical with the sport described in the *Bhāgavata-purāṇa*, except that in Goloka it is unmanifest. The Godhead, then, is not restful, silent, and still in its essence but is constantly and restlessly moving in self-delight and rambunctious play.

Another theological idea that underlines the blissful nature of the divine by stressing its warmth and approachability is the teaching that Bhagavān (the Lord) is a superior, more complete revelation of the divine than Brahman (the impersonal Absolute). This idea is as old as *bhakti* itself and was philosophically articulated as early as Rāmānuja. The object of the devotee's passionate service is not the attributeless, aloof Brahman of the *advaita* school. The devotee's object, rather, is God as infinitely qualified, infinitely blessed, the Lord Bhagavān. In Bengal Vaiṣṇava theology God is one but has a threefold aspect: Bhagavān, Paramātman, and Brahman. Paramātman is God in relation to nature *(prakṛti)* and spirit *(jīva)*, Brahman is unqualified and therefore never expressed, while Bhagavān is infinitely qualified

[27]This idea is also seen in the texts of the Vallabhācāryas.

The sacred Brindavana and Syam are eternal. Radha and the women of Braj also are eternal. . . . The happiness in the bowers is eternal and the gust of three kinds of wind also is eternal. Where Vasanta (Spring) also lives eternally and there is always pleasure and no sorrow. There the cuckoos and the parrots always make noise and the prepossessing beauty of the Lord like Kama is eternal. In the forest on the branches flowers of many kinds bloom up and the intoxicated black bees hum eternally. The beauty of the new leaves in the forest is unique, where many maidens enjoy in the company of Hari. The female cuckoo makes her cooing audible. The woman is pleased when she hears it.

(From Sūrdās' *Sūrsāgar*, in Misra, *The Religious Poetry of Surdas*, pp. 114–15.)

and infinitely perfect and is considered the most sublime aspect of all.[28] And Kṛṣṇa, finally, is identical with Bhagavān.

Turning to the inner dynamics of the Godhead, as articulated in Bengal Vaiṣṇava theology, we find a systematic attempt to articulate the essential nature of the divine as bliss. According to this system there are within the Godhead several *śaktis* (aspects or dimensions of the divine), the three most important of which are: *svarūpa-śakti, jīva-śakti,* and *māyā-śakti.* And within the *svarūpa-śakti* (the essential or "own" *śakti*) there are three more *śaktis*: *saṁdhīnī* (identified with *sat*), *saṁvit* (identified with *cit*), and *hlādinī* (identified with *ānanda,* although including also *sat* and *cit*). It is through his *śaktis* that the divine expresses himself. Through his *jīva-śakti* he expresses himself by creating individual souls, through his *māyā-śakti* he creates the world, and through his *svarūpa-śakti* he expresses his "own" form, his essential nature. All creations (or expressions) arising from his *svarūpa-śakti* are essentially the same as God, since they are entirely within his essential selfhood; they are intrinsically related to the Godhead, eternally existing within it. And what are the creations, or expressions, of the Godhead's *svarūpa-śakti*? They are the people of Vṛndāvana, especially the *gopīs*, and particularly Rādhā. The theological interpretation of the origin of Rādhā and the *gopīs* is important, for it declares that not just Kṛṣṇa alone, but also Kṛṣṇa surrounded by the population and paraphernalia of Vṛndāvana, is the essential form of the Godhead. The whole Vṛndāvana episode, then, is understood to take place *within the Godhead constantly.* In its essential form the Godhead is an eternal, playful, delightful dalliance in paradisiacal Vṛndāvana.[29]

[28]See De's discussion of Jīva Gosvāmin's *Bhagavat-saṁdarbha* for a concise treatment of this theological system *(Vaisnava Faith and Movement,* pp. 472–80).

[29]Girindra Narayan Mallik, *The Philosophy of Vaiṣṇava Religion* (Lahore: Punjab Sanskrit Book Depot, 1927), pp. 128–29.

The gradations of perfection or completeness within the *svarūpa-śakti* serve to underline the Godhead further as blissful in its most distilled essence. The most essential *śakti* (of the three within the *svarūpa-śakti*) is the *hlādinī-śakti*, which is pure bliss. And the *hlādinī-śakti* is none other than, and is identical with, Rādhā.[30] Kṛṣṇa, as the Godhead, not only expresses bliss in his essential form, then, but also enjoys it. Ever blissful in his essential form, he also tastes or enjoys bliss, as his innermost being is in reality an inner dalliance, the eternal love affair between Rādhā and himself. The Absolute, then, is an eternal love affair between God and himself (herself) that is played out forever with all its humor and tenderness, frenzy and abandon, pique and reconciliation.

The centrality of the *hlādinī-śakti,* and Rādhā's identification with it, underscore dramatically the sublimation of lordship to bliss in the Godhead. In Vṛndāvana, which is God's most perfect revelation (insofar as it is simply a making manifest of his eternal, essential form), Kṛṣṇa's lordship is in almost total abeyance.[31] In Vṛndāvana Kṛṣṇa is a son, companion, and lover. He does not dictate his will, govern from a throne, or behave in a lordly or mighty way. His sole occupation is to revel in bliss, to frisk about as if intoxicated. While lordship and awesome power certainly belong to the Godhead, its most essential nature is to infuse and taste bliss in the intimacy of love.[32]

[30]Prabodhānanda Sarasvatī, *Ānanda-vṛndāvana-campū* (Bengali) (n.p., n.d.) [title page missing; probably published late nineteenth century], p. 120. Rādhā was also identified with the *śakti* of Kṛṣṇa by Nimbārka and Vallabha (De, *Vaiṣnava Faith and Movement,* p. 7).

[31]This explains why in Bengal Vaiṣṇavism the two-armed form of Kṛṣṇa is considered superior to the four-armed or many-armed forms. The four-armed form suggests power and majesty, an aloofness that is not consistent with God's essential nature as bliss.

[32]A story in the *Bhaktamāl*, the Hindu book of saints, illustrates this well. A devotee named Bhabuk Brāhman lived in Vṛndāvana and worshiped Kṛṣṇa in the form of a child. He treated the god as his own son, feeding him, disciplining

Indian spirituality offers several paradigms of the divine or heroic spiritual achievement that suggest the placid, quietistic stillness of the transcendent other realm of the gods or the state of spiritual perfection. The withdrawn, meditating *yogin*, completely closed off from the phenomenal world in trance; the Jain Tīrthaṅkara, immobile, statuelike, and rigid; and the calm, unrippled countenance of the Buddha all suggest a vision of otherness that is beyond flux and becoming. These models convey the truth that the Absolute, or participation in the Absolute, is silent, still, and unchanging in its essence. The topsy-turvy world of Kṛṣṇa seems to suggest a different vision. Kṛṣṇa's realm is passionate, frenzied, and tumultuous. He is never still in his rambunctious play and intoxicating revelry.

In some ways, of course, the vision of Kṛṣṇa is different from the unchanging, eternal, silent reality of the visions expressed in the above paradigms. But Kṛṣṇa's topsy-turvy world is also in tune with these visions of stillness. For, insofar as Kṛṣṇa expresses himself most completely in Vṛndāvana, he reveals the truth (also underlying the "still" visions) that the divine does not express itself in any essential way through history, nature, or creation-maintenance-destruction of the world. In a real sense Kṛṣṇa does not act at all in Vṛüdāvana. In Vṛndāvana he simply *is*. From the standpoint of Bengal Vaiṣṇava theology, or from the point of view of the devotee of Kṛṣṇa the cowherd, Kṛṣṇa simply displays himself in Vṛndāvana. He has no mission, seeks no prestige or power; he simply overflows himself. He

---

him, and playing with him. One day, however, the devotee was possessed by the thought that the image he worshiped as his own son was actually the supreme God, and he suddenly had feelings of awe and servitude toward him. He lost his feeling of parental affection for Kṛṣṇa and prayed to him, blessing his majesty and power. As soon as this happened, Kṛṣṇa disappeared, reprimanding Bhabuk Brāhman for his loss of love for God as a child. With the appearance of distance between the devotee and Kṛṣṇa came the disappearance of the god (Nābha Dās, *Bhaktamāl,* ed. Upendranāth Mukherji, translated into Bengali by Kṛṣnadas Babaji [n.p.: Basumatī Sāhitya Mandir, 1924], pp. 143–44).

does not reveal himself so much as he displays himself. He does not act decisively in a historical, moral, or cosmic sense. He simply lifts the curtain, as it were, on his innermost being, which is revealed to be self-delight. He reveals the Godhead to be unconcerned with and aloof from the world, totally immersed in its own dazzling beauty. The essential nature of the divine is shown to "exert" itself for no pragmatic purpose. It is shown to revel in its own incomparably joyful being by playing with itself, making love to itself, inciting itself to abandon itself in itself. Kṛṣṇa, the playful, charming cowherd boy who sports in Vṛndāvana, expresses the truth that the divine is most completely itself when it dallies aimlessly, overflowing itself in self-delight and self-generated rapture.

Līlā: The Divine Player

Another important Hindu theme that underlies and is articulated by the vision of the cowherd Kṛṣṇa is *līlā*, divine play, sport, or dalliance. *Līlā* is descriptive of divine activity in Hinduism in at least two ways. First, it underlines the completeness of the gods. The gods need and desire nothing, yet they continue to act. In the *Bhagavadgītā* Kṛṣṇa himself says to Arjuna:

> For Me, son of Pṛthā, there is nothing to be done
> In the three worlds whatsoever,
> Nothing unattained to be attained;
> And yet I still continue in action.[33]

Because the gods are complete and therefore do not act according to pragmatic laws of cause and effect to fulfill this or that desire, their actions are called play. The gods by their nature do not work, for to work is to fulfill some need or shortcoming. In their completeness their actions can only be called play. As players, then,

[33] *Bhagavadgītā* 3. 22 (p. 20).

the gods are understood to be aloof from the world. They create the world in play and involve themselves only incidentally or accidentally with the ongoing world order. They do not complete themselves in the creation, maintenance, or destruction of the world, they simply amuse and display themselves. Their actions, as such, are not "serious"; they are without calculation and premeditation, superfluous vis-à-vis the divine economy. The actions of the gods (as play) are not capricious but transcendent in their aloofness.

Līlā is descriptive of divine activity in another way. The gods as players are revealed to act spontaneously, unpredictably, and sometimes tumultuously. To play is to be unfettered and unconditioned, to perform actions that are intrinsically satisfying: to sing, dance, and laugh. To play is to step out of the ordinary world of the humdrum, to enter a special, magical world where one can revel in the superfluous. To play is to display oneself aimlessly and gracefully. As players, then, the gods are revealed to be delightful, joyful, graceful beings whose actions are completely spontaneous, unconditioned, and expressive of their transcendent completeness and freedom. No Hindu deity expresses this aspect of the divine more completely than the cowherd Kṛṣṇa.[34]

It is clear from what has already been said about Kṛṣṇa that his entire life among the cowherds of Vṛndāvana is play. As a child he and Balarāma scamper around the cowherd town rolling in the dust, dancing, and laughing to the delight of their parents. Kṛṣṇa expresses the transcendent freedom and spontaneity of the divine by romping about the village completely undeterred by social or parental restrictions. He unties the cows, steals butter and sweets, and wakes up sleeping infants. As a child he is uncontrollable, the expert player. As an adolescent he joins with

[34]For the importance of play in Hindu mythology and its relationship to other Hindu themes, see David Kinsley, "The Divine Player: A Study of Kṛṣṇa-līlā" (Ph.D. diss., Divinity School, University of Chicago, 1970), pp. 7–84.

his band of cowherd companions and expresses the wilder aspects of play. He runs, jumps, and bounds through the forests of Vṛndāvana expressing the irrepressible, anarchical, tumultuous enthusiasm of youth. When demons appear and seek to intrude upon his magic world of play, his play does not stop but continues right through the contest. His play is not curbed in any way by these demons, and his mood is in no way sobered; his play simply expresses itself in a different way, in playful combat. As the lover of the *gopīs* Kṛṣṇa pervades the bowers of Vṛndāvana and the banks and waters of the Jumna River with a carnival atmosphere. Frolicking, dancing, and making love with the *gopīs*, he incites them to frenzy and abandon. The world of social responsibility is left behind. The moral laws of the humdrum world are held in abeyance in the magic world of Kṛṣṇa's dalliance. Within the idyllic, magic circle of love the extraordinary is ordinary; freedom and joy reign in Kṛṣṇa's Garden of Eden. In response to the irresistible call of his flute, the *gopīs* leave their husbands and children to rush to the forest to be with their darling. The gods are incapable of resisting its call and are drawn to Vṛndāvana. Nature blossoms, thrills, and celebrates in response to its intoxicating sound. Tumult and frenzy pervade Vṛndāvana's sanctuary of romantic and erotic dalliance. The day-to-day world is forgotten and transcended, and Kṛṣṇa's consorts revel in bliss.

Kṛṣṇa's entire sojourn in Vṛndāvana serves no "purpose." According to the *Harivaṁśa*, *Viṣṇu-purāṇa*, and *Bhāgavata-purāṇa* Viṣṇu incarnates himself as Kṛṣṇa when Mother Earth requests him to relieve her of the tyrannical burden of the demon-king Kaṁsa. Kṛṣṇa's life in Vṛndāvana, however, proceeds with hardly any reference to this mission. Only when demons appear, in most cases sent by Kaṁsa to kill the child, are we reminded of Kṛṣṇa's ostensible mission. The way in which Kṛṣṇa deals with these adversaries, however, does not break the mood of playful freedom that fills Vṛndāvana while Kṛṣṇa is there. His life in Vṛndāvana is sheer dalliance, superfluous vis-à-vis his mission as Viṣṇu's *avatāra*. Its raison d'être (if the term may be applied at all) is aimless display. In Vṛndāvana Kṛṣṇa is removed from the ordinary world and the necessity of acting according to pragmatic considerations. In Vṛndāvana he need not play a role but is free to express his essential nature in every action. In the cowherd village, removed from the world of his mission as an *avatāra*, there are no inhibitions to acting freely. Vṛndāvana is a playground, a magic place, where Kṛṣṇa can revel freely and continually as a playful child. Vṛndāvana is the Garden before the Fall, a place in which man and God may mingle freely and intimately in playful abandon. In this atmosphere God's essential nature, the divine, in the form of the beautiful cowherd Kṛṣṇa, may express itself in play and self-delight.

Kṛṣṇa's long history is nearly as old as Hinduism itself, and over the centuries he has been many things to many people. He has been a counselor, companion, politician, teacher, king, and Bhagavāvan, the Lord. But it was as a humble cowherd boy that he was destined to gain his immense popularity and fame. From Kṛṣṇa's long and detailed history, from his elaborate Purāṇic biography, it is striking that the medieval *bhakti* cults of the North (those of Nimbārka, Vallabha, and Caitanya) have focused on Kṛṣṇa's superfluous life as a youth in Vṛndāvana to the almost total exclusion of the rest of his history and biography. In these cults his idyllic life there has been bracketed, as it were, and extolled as his most complete manifestation. His sojourn in Vṛndāvana in effect has been taken from its biographical context and made into the be-all and end-all of his manifestation. His later biography is seen as an insignificant epilogue compared to his life in Vṛndāvana. Dvārkā (the city in which Kṛṣṇa lives during the latter part of his life) is not important as the seat of his kingly rule and courtly life. It is primarily a synonym for his absence when Rādhā and the *gopīs* sing their threnodies of love in separation. In attempting to understand why the most frivolous and apparently inconsequential chapter of Kṛṣṇa's biography has been fastened upon as the most meaningful by the medieval *bhakti* cults, I would refer to a popular Bengali saying: "Without Kṛṣṇa there is no song" ("kānu binā gīta nāhi").

In the teeming Hindu pantheon there are several gods who excel at making the world whirl in the maddening rhythms of creation, maintenance, and destruction. There are gods whose heavens are merry sporting grounds, whose days are spent in amorous dalliance with dancing *apsarases* and singing *gandharvas.* There are intoxicated and intoxicating gods who seem insane in their tumultuous, reckless adventures. There are great magicians among the gods who conjure up dizzying creations to amuse themselves and stupify others. There are beautiful gods and goddesses, gods who sing and laugh and dance. There are many gods who play.

But "without Kṛṣṇa," the Bengali verse says, "there is no song." For of all the Hindu gods Kṛṣṇa expresses most completely all that is beautiful, graceful, and enticing in the other world of the divine. He embodies all those things that are extra in life, all those luxuries and characteristics that are not necessary to life but without which life would not be worth living. He is witty, gay, careless, accomplished at dancing, singing, and playing the flute. He is loved with abandon and loves with abandon. He is surpassingly beautiful. He is irresistibly and bewitchingly charming. All that he does is executed with effortless grace and harmony. And though he is an immensely powerful being, he is not haughty or proud, vindictive or jealous. He does not live in a palace, he does not sit in majesty upon a throne. His heavenly court is held in the glades and bowers of Vṛndāvana, where he sports as an equal with lowly cowherd women or plays with cowherd boys. His appearance is not mighty but almost rustic. He runs, jumps, scampers, and bounds through the forest in a constant display of irrespressible vitality and enthusiasm. His entire life at Vṛndāvana "accomplishes" nothing. It is frivolous, purposeless. His essential qualities as a cowherd youth are not those that would lend themselves to an orderly, pious routine in the normal, pragmatic world. His essential qualities are "mere" adornments. His beauty, humor, artistic talent, and playful spirit are ornamental, intended only for aimless display. And it is precisely these extra qualities, his ornamental nature, that set him apart from the world of the ordinary and express the essence of the divine world of the other. He is the embodiment of all that is implied in the word *līlā*: light, almost aerial activity, boisterous revelry, frivolity, spontaneity, and freedom.

In Vṛndāvana Kṛṣṇa's life is a continuous song, a melodious, harmonious symphony of beauty, grace, and joy. Here God plays, losing himself in ecstatic, spontaneous revelry. Here life is a celebration, not a duty. Here life does not grind along but scampers in dance and rejoices in song. All that makes life in the pragmatic world endurable is to be found here. This is the other world of the divine, from which beauty, freedom, and bounty proceed. Here the bondage of necessity does not exist. Kṛṣṇa is here, filling the world with the melody of his flute. And those who have heard it say: "Without Kṛṣṇa there is no song."

PART II

THE SWORD: KĀLĪ, MISTRESS OF DEATH

CHAPTER III

INTRODUCTION

There are two general matters that should be discussed before dealing with the history and meaning of the goddess Kālī. The first has to do with her extreme appearance and her dubious associations. The second concerns her relationship to the Hindu "Great Tradition." In both matters I bring certain assumptions to this study that should be made clear at the outset.

Probably no Hindu deity has been more frequently maligned, by both non-Hindus and Hindus,[1] than Kālī. In large measure this has been the result of her terrifying appearance, which strikes many observers as extreme.

> She is dark as a great cloud, clad in dark clothes. Her tongue is poised as if to lick. She has fearful teeth, sunken eyes, and is smiling. She wears a necklace of snakes, the half-moon rests on her forehead, she has matted hair, and is engaged in licking a corpse. Her sacred thread is a snake, and she lies on a bed of snakes. She holds a garland of fifty heads. She has a large belly, and on her head is Ananta with a thousand heads. On all sides she is surrounded by snakes. . . . She has a snake-girdle and an anklet of jewels. On her left is to be imagined Śiva in the form of a boy. She has two hands and has corpses for ear ornaments. Her face, decked with bright, new jewels, shows she is pleased and calm.[2]

It is sometimes said that Indian culture generally betrays a love for extremes, that moderation and balance tend to get lost

[1]Even such famous Bengali literary figures as Rabindranath Tagore and Bankim Chatterjee, whom one could expect to have a sympathetic view of Kālī, were highly suspicious of her and tended to interpret her negatively. Tagore's drama *Sacrifice* is a clear denunciation of her cult, while Chatterjee's *Kopal-kuṇḍala* tends to see in Kālī not a redeeming figure but primarily a goddess who belonged to the fringes of society.

[2]The *dhyāna mantra* of *guhya-kālī* from Kṛṣṇānanda Āgamavāgīśa's *Tantrasāra* (1:326).

in the Indian tendency to press everything to its ultimate limit. Heinrich Zimmer, for example, says that a typical feature of Indian art is "that amazing tendency to go to the very limits of delight and terror, and even to press almost beyond them, in the representation both of the wonders of the world's sensual charm and of the hair-raising, horrifying aspects of destructive forces."[3]

Whether or not the goddess Kālī is illustrative of such a general trait in the Indian character, she does appear to represent a presence that dramatically and unambiguously confronts one with "the hair-raising, horrifying aspects" of reality. She represents, it seems, something that has been pushed to its ultimate limits, something that has been apprehended as unspeakably terrifying, something totally and irreconcilably "other." She seems "extreme."

Kālī's associations with blood sacrifice (sometimes human), her position as patron goddess of the infamous Thugs, and her importance in Vāmācāra Tantric ritual have generally won for her a reputation as a creature born of a crazed, aboriginal mind. She seems, in the words of an awestruck writer at the beginning of this century, "to have somehow blundered into the daylight of the twentieth century, . . . unmodified by time and unsoftened by culture."[4] Even when compared with Śiva's *ghora* (terrible) forms, Kālī stands out as a creature who is wild, frantic, out of control. And if it were not for her extraordinary popularity in the Hindu tradition, we might be able to say, as impartial students of religious man, that she is an "extreme case," an aberration, a dark, frightening creature conjured up by a few who existed on the fringes of Indian society—that she is interesting and remarkable, but irrelevant to the mainstream of Indian religious thought.

[3]Heinrich Zimmer, *The Art of Indian Asia,* ed. Joseph Campbell (New York: Pantheon Books, 1955), 1:135.

[4]J. C. Oman, *The Brahmanas, Theists and Muslims of India* (London: T. Fisher Unwin, 1907), p. 22.

A presupposition of this study, however, is that Kālī, as one of the most popular Hindu divinities (in Bengal, at least), says something fundamental about the Hindu vision of things. It is assumed at the outset that Kālī sums up certain truths of the tradition. By briefly considering her history, mythology, and iconography, I shall seek to discern what those truths might be.

The second general matter I wish to discuss concerns the problem of the "Great" (sometimes called "Indo-Aryan," "brāhmanic," "Vedic," or "orthodox") and "little" (sometimes called "Dravidian," "tribal," "indigenous," or "regional") traditions in India and the historical framework within which Kālī should be understood. The issue is a perennial one for Indian scholarship and has led to two differing attempts to locate such deities as Kālī (who do not appear in the tradition till post-Vedic times) in the overall tradition.

At one extreme there are those who would see in Kālī simply a manifestation of a "Great Goddess," an amorphous being at best who reveals herself as early as the *Ṛg-veda* as Pṛthivī (the earth), Uṣas (the dawn), Aditi,[5] Rātrī, or some other goddess with whom Kālī has very little in common.[6] The assumption seems to be that there existed in Vedic India a being comparable to figures in the ancient Near East or the Mediterranean area,[7] although such a being does not actually make her appearance

[5]E. Washburn Hopkins, for example, says; "All these forms of Uma (= Amma, the great mother-goddess) go back to the primitive and universal cult of the mother-goddess (cf. Aditi)" (*Epic Mythology* [Varanasi: Indological Book House, 1968], p. 226). He is speaking here of Kālī and other goddesses who appear in the *Mahābhārata*.

[6]The only goddess who appears in Vedic literature who shares important characteristics with Kālī is Nirṛti. Nirṛti and other possible prototypes of Kālī in early literature are discussed below.

[7]J. Przyluski's "The Great Goddess of India and Iran," *Indian Historical Quarterly* 10 (1934): 405–30, and S. K. Dikshit's *The Mother Goddess (A Study in the Origin of Hinduism)* (Poona: International Book Service, n.d.) are examples of this approach.

in the *Ṛg-veda.*[8] Another assumption underlying this approach seems to be that femaleness is an essentially defining characteristic of any goddess. That is, if two otherwise completely differing deities are both feminine, then it is held (on grounds that are never made clear) that they must be reducible to manifestations of one "Great Goddess." It would seem that femaleness alone (and not maleness) is used as such a defining characteristic, for the male beings of the tradition are recognized as individual beings in their own right. To my knowledge no one has yet come up with a "Great God" theory to explain the differences between early and late male deities in the Hindu tradition. No one, for example, has tried to show that Ganeśa, Kṛṣṇa, Rāma, or Kārttikeya (all popular in the later tradition but absent from the Vedic literature) are really manifestations of a "Great God" who manifests himself in the *Ṛg-veda* as Iṅdra, Agni, Varuna, or the like. To do the same thing with Kālī is equally unjustified. Kālī can be shown to have an identity of her own, quite distinct from all other deities in the tradition, and this identity may not be reduced to her sex.

At the other extreme is the interpretation of Kālī that insists on her essentially indigenous, non-Aryan character throughout her history. In support of this interpretation it is clear that most

[8]The "Devi," or "Mahādevī" (the "Great Goddess"), does appear in later literature, particularly in the *Purāṇas,* and there is a conscious attempt at this time to subsume all goddesses under her in several scriptures (*e.g.*, the *Devī-māhātmya*, which I discuss below; the *Saundaryalaharī*, attributed to Śaṅkara, but written somewhat later, and the *Lalitā-sahasranām*, a part of the *Brahmāṇḍa-purāṇa*). It is as unfair to read the synchronizing tendencies of later Hinduism in respect to the Great Goddess back into Vedic literature, however, as it is to read the Trimūrti of Brahmā-Viṣṇu-Śiva back into the *Vedas*. Even in later Hinduism it is important to distinguish between epithets, *avatāras*, and aspects of various deities. While it is quite clear, for example, that Kālī in many texts is said to arise from Durgā or to represent the dynamic aspect of Śiva, she cannot possibly be understood simply in relation to these deities. Kālī, quite clearly, is a being in her own right, and no attempt to subsume her under another, perhaps more powerful or greater, deity can hide that fact.

early references to Kālī associate her with tribal groups living on the periphery of Indian society. It is also clear that Kālī is still regarded with suspicion by many in the Hindu tradition; her popularity in Bengal, never known for its orthodoxy, further suggests her essentially indigenous character. While Kālī's association with tribal, indigenous peoples[9] cannot be denied, her subsequent popularity in the tradition cannot be explained simply from this point of view. To say that the Hindu tradition, for social or political reasons, recognized Kālī as another manifestation of Durgā or the Great Goddess (Devī) does not explain her rise to prominence. It is well known that the brāhmanic tradition for various reasons accepted into its fold (either willingly or unwillingly) many indigenous deities and customs. In just this way the Aryan tradition was able to accommodate very diverse peoples among the indigenous population. But at some point Kālī ceases to be an indigenous, tribal goddess, associated with the periphery of society, and begins to gain an amazing prominence in the pantheon. At this point, I think, one has to recognize the fact that Kālī has become a Hindu goddess, expressing the Hindu vision of things in her own way. The point is that Kālī's origins do not and cannot adequately explain her subsequent history. She eventually transcends her origins.

The history of Kālī as presented here, then, will not insist exclusively upon either her disguised presence in the tradition from the very beginning or her essentially indigenous, tribal nature in her eventual rise to popularity. To do the former is to compromise the integrity of Kālī as a goddess in her own right, and to do the latter is to ignore her eventual "at homeness" in the Hindu pantheon. In sketching the history of this goddess, two things about her must be consistently acknowledged. First, Kālī expresses truths of the tradition. She is today in India a

[9]There is no convincing evidence that Kālī, or a goddess resembling Kālī, was known in the Indus Valley civilization, although there is abundant evidence of the worship of feminine deities.

well-known goddess whose mythology and iconography underline important Hindu themes. To insist upon her essentially tribal, peripheral aspects or her current Bengali associations, ignoring her popularity throughout India, is to misunderstand her meaning to the tradition. Second, Kālī from her earliest appearances in the tradition to the present time has had a discernible identity in her own right. Kālī's history, once she is recognized by the tradition, is not simply a process of making her name an epithet of another goddess or her appearance an aspect of another goddess, although both of these things can be demonstrated to have taken place to some extent. Kālī does not make her way in the tradition solely on the basis of conflation with other goddesses; she makes her way in her own right. Her appearance changes, to be sure, as she rises in importance, but her essential nature remains identifiable throughout her long history. In other words, Kālī keeps her integrity despite various changes in appearance and function. She is not simply "used" by the Great Tradition: she brings something to that tradition, revealing herself to that tradition, and it is not an exaggeration to say that in this process the tradition itself is enriched.

The Prehistory of Kālī

Kālī has not always been known to the literary or Great Tradition of India. Her appearance in the tradition as a goddess having a cycle of myths and a consistent description does not occur until the epic and Purāṇic periods (circa 200 B.C. to A.D. 300). This is not to say that Kālī was not known outside the literary tradition (among tribal peoples, for example) prior to the time of the epics and the *Purāṇas*. There is evidence, in fact, that she was.

The name Kālī appears in earlier literature. In *Muṇḍaka Upaniṣad* 1. 2. 4 it is one of the names of the seven tongues of Agni. Since Kālī is later associated with destruction and the cremation ground, it might be supposed that this early text forms the basis for the later, fully developed goddess. However, it is dangerous to read too much into this reference, which in context is simply a description of the sacrificial fire. There is no clear indication that the first six names of Agni's tongues are to be taken as representing actual beings.

Among possible prototypes of Kālī in early literature are Rātrīdevī (the goddess Night) and the demoness Nirṛti. As Kālī is later associated with the night and is sometimes referred to as the "terrible night of destruction," a continuity between Rātrīdevī and Kālī might be postulated. Rātrī's general description, however, does not convey the image of a terrible being like Kālī (for example, *Ṛg-veda* X. 127). She is closely identified with darkness, to be sure, but she is supplicated as the sister of Dawn, Uṣas, and the impression one gets from *Ṛg-veda* X. 127 is that she is a benign figure. Any continuity she might have with the later Kālī seems tenuous.

The demoness Nirṛti is frequently mentioned in Vedic literature. She appears to be the personification of death, destruction, and sorrow, and whenever she is addressed the intent of the *mantra* is to ward her off (for example, *Ṛg-veda* X. 59. 1–4; VII. 37. 7; *Atharva-veda* II. 10. 4–8; IV. 36. 10; VI. 29. 2). She is said to wear dark clothes, receive dark husks as her sacrificial portion, and have a dark complexion (*Taittirīya-brāhmaṇa* I. 6. 1. 4). She lives in the South, the direction of Yama and the abode of death (*Śatapatha-brāhmaṇa* V. 2. 3. 3). In general Nirṛti bears a striking resemblance to Kālī: they are both dark, dread goddesses associated with suffering, misfortune, and death. There are, nevertheless, important differences between them. Kālī plays an active role as a warrior goddess and receives blood sacrifices, while Nirṛti does neither. Kālī is usually described as naked, with lolling tongue and fanglike teeth, while Nirṛti is clothed. Kālī is always said to have black, disheveled hair, while Nirṛti is described in *Atharva-veda* V. 7. 9 as "golden-locked." It is doubtful, therefore, that the two goddesses can be identified.[10] Nirṛti almost entirely disappears from the tradition at approximately the time that Kālī begins to be known; Nirṛti is rarely mentioned in the epic-Purāṇic texts. It seems that functionally the two goddesses are much alike, both being to some extent personifications of death and sorrow, and it is probable that in Kālī the Great Tradition saw many of the same things that it saw in Nirṛti. Nowhere have I been able to find the two identified, however, and it is most likely that the two cannot be linked historically. Particularly in her early history, Kālī is identified as a tribal goddess who is worshiped by hunters or thieves. She makes her "debut" in the Great Tradition in a battle context, and in that context she is described quite differently from Nirṛti. Perhaps the most that can be said is that the Great Tradition was at least partially receptive to Kālī insofar as she affirmed certain realities conveyed earlier by Nirṛti. Her way into the tradition had been partially prepared for her, as it were, by Nirṛti.

Kālī in the Mahābhārata

There are only a few passages in the *Mahābhārata* that mention Kālī.[11] In Sabhā Parva (11. 29) she is named as one of those beings who live in Brahmā's heaven. No description is given of her, however. In Śalya Parva (45. 11, 13) Bhadrakālī and Kālikā are given as names of two of the "mothers" who became the

[10]Sukumari Bhattacharji's *The Indian Theogony* (Cambridge: Cambridge University Press, 1970) has a good summary of Nirṛti's appearance and place in Indian literature. Her hypothesis is that Nirṛti's functions are replaced by Kālī, Karālī, Cāmuṇḍā, and Chinnamastā—that essentially these later, terrible goddesses are direct descendents of Nirṛti (p. 85). This is in line with her general argument, which tries to demonstrate how most later Hindu deities are by and large the old Vedic gods in new disguises and roles, an argument I do not find convincing in most cases.

[11]Only references to Kālī in the critical edition of the *Mahābhārata* will be discussed at this point (ed. Vishnu S. Sukthankar et al. [Poona: Bhandarkar Oriental Research Institute, 1933]).

companions of Kārttikeya (Skanda or Kumāra) when he went forth to slay the demon Tāraka. The mothers collectively are said to be both beautiful and terrifying and are said to live in trees, caves, mountains, crossroads, and cremation grounds. They are said to wear various kinds of clothes, to speak different languages, and some are said to be dark in color (45. 38–39). The names of the mothers are all given in a long list without individual descriptions. The above characteristics are then suggested for various beings among the group as a whole, although specific names are not mentioned in connection with specific characteristics. The implication seems to be, however, that generally these goddesses (Kālī included) are associated with peripheral places and non-Aryan peoples (insofar as they speak different languages).

The most important reference to Kālī in the epic is in Sauptika Parva 8. 65–68. Kālī appears after the sleeping Pāṇḍava army has been treacherously slaughtered by the Kaurava warriors Aśvatthāmā, Kṛpa, and Kṛtavarma (the only survivors from the Kaurava side after the great battle of Kurukṣetra). As in later descriptions she is black, her mouth is bloody, her hair is disheveled, and she holds a noose with which she leads the dead away.[12]

In summary, the few passages that mention Kālī in the *Mahābhārata* tell us little about her. She is associated with a group of goddesses (the *mātṛkās*) who seem to be peripheral or non-Aryan deities and companions of Kārttikeya (himself a fairly late Hindu god). She is associated, further, with death and destruction, but nothing of her mythology is told. There is no indication that

[12]The two well-known hymns in praise of Durgā (Bhīsma Parva 23 and Virāta Parva 6) and the episode concerning Dakṣa's sacrifice, in which Kālī is created from Umā's wrath (Śānti Parva 284. 32, 54 [Appendix 1. 28. 1–247 of Śānti Parva in the critical edition]), are not found in the critical edition of the *Mahābhārata* and appear to be interpolations, coming from a time contemporary with or later than the *Devī-māhātmya*. These passages, therefore, are not discussed here. For the date of these passages, see B. C. Mazumdar, "Durga: Her Origin and History," *Journal of the Royal Asiatic Society of Great Britain* 38 (1906–7): 355–58.

she is identified with any male deity or major female deity, nor is there any hint of the kind of worship she receives or what kinds of people might be included among her devotees. Only in passages not included in the critical edition of the *Mahābhārata* is she associated with Durgā, Śiva, or Viṣṇu. It seems clear that during the epic period, and throughout the period of its compilation into its present form (400 B.C. to A.D. 400), Kālī was not recognized as a major Hindu deity, was not yet identified with any deity in the established pantheon, and existed as a very minor deity on the fringes of the tradition. We must turn to the *Devī-māhātmya* of the *Mārkaṇḍeya-purāṇa* for further information about Kālī.

Kālī in the Devī-māhātmya

In the *Devī-māhātmya* a full account of the goddess Kālī is given.[13] Her birth, appearance, and central mythological deeds are told in detail. It is in this text that Kālī, as she came to be known in the tradition, makes her debut, her official entrance into the Great Tradition of Hinduism. The *Devī-māhātmya* is divided into three major episodes. In the first two episodes the Devī, the Great Goddess, or Durgā, as she is called frequently here, defeats the demons Kaiṭabha and Madhu (both born from Viṣṇu during his cosmic sleep) and the great demon Mahiṣāsura. It is during the third episode, in which the Goddess confronts the demon brothers Śumbha and Niśumbha and their army, that Kālī appears. Śumbha and Niśumbha have subdued the gods and now rule over them. The gods have collectively petitioned the Great Goddess

[13]The *Devī-māhātmya* is a separate and complete composition despite the fact that it is found inserted in the *Mārkaṇḍeya-purāṇa* (chaps. 81–93). It is treated as a separate scripture by worshipers of the Goddess and is printed as a separate text throughout India. The text is popularly known as the *Caṇḍī* (one of the names of the Goddess) and the *Saptasatī*, "the seven hundred" (a reference to the number of verses in the *Devī-māhātmya*, although it actually has somewhat fewer verses than this).

(who previously had promised to assist them whenever they found themselves in difficulty), and she has appeared in the guise of Pārvatī, from whom she emerges and presents herself in all her magnificence (85. 37–40). She calms the worried throng of gods and goes forth to battle the demon hosts. The first demon heroes sent forth to battle her are Caṇḍa and Muṇḍa. When they approach Durgā with drawn swords and bent bows, she becomes furious, her face becoming dark as ink. Suddenly there springs forth from her brow the terrible goddess Kālī, armed with a sword and noose. She is adorned with a garland of human heads, wears a tiger's skin, and waves a staff with a skull handle. She is gaunt, with sunken, reddish eyes, gaping mouth, lolling tongue and emaciated flesh. She fills the four quarters with her terrifying roar and leaps eagerly into the fray. She flings demons into her mouth and crushes them in her jaws. She wades through the demon hosts, decapitating and crushing all who stand before her. Laughing and howling loudly, she approaches Caṇḍa and Muṇḍa, grasps them by the hair, and in one furious instant decapitates them both with her mighty sword. Returning to Durgā with the two heads, she laughs jokingly and presents them to the Goddess as a gift.[14]

A second incident in this cosmic battle features Kālī. The demon army has nearly been defeated. But there remains the fearful demon Raktabīja. This demon is nearly invincible, for every time he is wounded and begins to bleed, other demons in

[14]*Mārkaṇḍeya-purāṇa* 87. 5–23. The entire *Mārkaṇḍeya-purāṇa* has been translated into English: *The Mārkaṇḍeya Purāṇa*, trans. F. Eden Pargiter (Delhi: Indological Book House, 1969). The *Devī-māhātmya* section has been translated separately: *Devī-māhātmyam: The Glorification of the Great Goddess*, trans. Vasudeva S. Agrawala (Varanasi: All-India Kashiraj Trust, 1963). The numbering of the chapters and verses in Agrawala's text does not correspond to the *Mārkaṇḍeya-purāṇa*, since he is treating the *Devī-māhātmya* as a separate scripture. In his text, therefore, chapter 1 corresponds to chapter 81 in the *Mārkaṇḍeya-purāṇa*, and so on through chapter 13, which corresponds to chapter 93. Throughout this discussion I use the chapter numbers of the *Mārkaṇḍeya-purāṇa*.

his image and with his might and ability to reproduce are instantly born from his blood. Durgā repeatedly strikes him with arrows and cuts him with her sword but soon realizes the situation is thereby becoming worse. She calls upon Kālī to defeat the monster. Kālī swoops onto the field of battle and opens her gigantic mouth. She swallows the blood-born creatures and drinks up the blood from Raktabīja's wounds. Finally, she sucks the blood from the demon, who falls to the ground dead.[15]

So Kālī makes her official appearance on the Hindu scene.[16] She is born from wrath, is horrible in appearance, and is ferocious in battle. Taking delight in destruction and death, she epitomizes the wild, fearful aspects of the divine. Her role in this scripture is clearly defined: she is subservient to the goddess Durgā and is called upon to help or rescue the Great Goddess in particularly

[15]88. 52–59. Cf. the Thuggee version of this myth: Francis Tuker, *The Yellow Scarf* (London: J. M. Dent & Sons, 1961), p. 62. In that version, Kālī, along with a horde of creatures she has created for the purpose, strangles these blood-born beings, thus killing them bloodlessly. As a reward for their help, Kālī instructs her creatures (the mythical forefathers of the Thugs) to make their living by strangling.

[16]As has been pointed out, Kālī was known to the Great Tradition prior to her appearance in the *Mārkaṇḍeya-purāṇa* (as the references to her in the *Mahābhārata* indicate). It is also most probable that she was worshiped by several tribes or "little cultures" long before her debut in the *Mārkaṇḍeya-purāṇa* and, indeed, that she was originally a tribal goddess of some kind. In the *Mārkaṇḍeya-purāṇa,* though, there is a conscious attempt to link her with the so-called Great Goddess and to identify her with a goddess named Cāmuṇḍa (87. 25). In this sense we can speak of her debut, or her "birth," vis-à-vis the Great Tradition of Hinduism. Just what her pre-Purāṇic history was is difficult, if not impossible, to determine. See Śaśibhūsan Dāsgupta, *Bhārater Śakti-sādhana o Śākta Sāhitya* (Bengali) (Calcutta: Sāhitya Saṅgsad, 1367 B.S. [1961]), pp. 63–89, for some theories about Kālī's prehistory and the various strands that have merged in this scripture. See also N. N. Bhattacharyya, *Indian Mother Goddess* (Calcutta: R. D. Press, 1971), pp. 54–56, for a discussion of Kālī and other "bloodthirsty" goddesses in the Indian tradition. Both of these scholars suggest that Kālī was originally an indigenous goddess worshiped with blood sacrifice by "wild" tribes such as the Śabaras.

difficult circumstances. Kālī proceeds from the Goddess and is finally withdrawn into the Goddess (90. 4).

The goddess Kālī who is worshiped in India today (primarily in Bengal) is obviously the same goddess who is born in the *Devī-māhātmya*. In appearance she is little changed. As a total symbol of the divine, however, she has gained independence from Durgā: she is the object of fervent devotion, her character has become richer and more complex, indeed she has come to represent for millions the highest manifestation of the divine in India. How Kālī succeeded in achieving this status, how she grew from a helper of Durgā, an embodiment of her wrath who played a subservient role, to mistress of the universe, the Mother of all, is extremely difficult to determine. Nevertheless, it seems clear that at least three major factors combined to bring about this change: (1) a growing Kālī mythology that soon associated her with the god Śiva, (2) her popularity in Tantrism, particularly the Hindu Vāmācāra Tantric tradition, and (3) the fervent devotion of a few Bengali poet-saints. These three factors, I think, were largely responsible for "completing" the image of Kālī as contained in the *Devī-māhātmya* in such a way that she could become what she is today for millions of her devotees.

The Early History of Kālī in Purānic and Dramatic Literature

Kālī's development into a major Hindu deity does not seem to have taken place immediately. Indeed, it seems that her acceptance was often reluctant and grudging. In much of the literature immediately following the *Devī-māhātmya* or roughly contemporary with it, Kālī continues to be either a servant of Durgā's, a particularly ferocious and minor manifestation of the Devī, or a purely negative, dark, and terrible fiend worshiped only by wild tribes or thieves.

In the *Agni-* and *Garuḍa-purāṇas* she is summoned in *mantras* invoked for success in war and against enemies generally. Her appearance is terrible, and her *mantras* are generally spine-chilling. She is gaunt, has fangs, laughs diabolically, dances frantically, wears a garland of corpses, sits on the back of a giant ghost, lives in the cremation ground, and is asked to crush, trample, break, and burn the enemy.[17]

In the *Bhāgavata-purāṇa* she is the patron goddess of a band of thieves (an association that she was to keep, as her identification with the Thugs demonstrates). The leader of the thieves seeks to gain her blessing so that he might be granted a son, and he captures a childlike, innocent *brāhman* to sacrifice to her. The effulgence of the saintly *brāhman*, however, scorches Kālī who leaps from her image and slaughters the band of thieves. She is described in the usual way: she has a dreadful face, large teeth, and laughs wildly. She and her following of demons decapitate all the thieves, become inebriated from drinking their blood, and begin to throw their heads around in sport.[18]

There are several references to terrible, bloodthirsty goddesses in the dramatic literature of about this time. Kālī herself is mentioned in Kālidāsa's *Kumārasaṁbhava* (7. 39), and it is clear (despite the poet's name) that during his time (fourth to fifth centuries A.D) she was still a quite minor deity. She is mentioned along with many other gods as part of Śiva's wedding procession. She brings up the rear, following a group of goddesses called the *mātṛkās* (mothers) and is said to wear a necklace of skulls.

In Subandhu's *Vāsavadattā* (sixth or seventh century A.D.) a goddess named Bhagavatī or Kātyāyanī is mentioned, and her description is much like Kālī's. She is said to have slain Śumbha

[17]*Agni-purāṇa* 133, 134, and 136; *Garuḍa-purāṇa* 38.

[18]*Bhāgavata-purāṇa* 5. 9. 12–20.

and Niśumbha,[19] to live on the banks of the Ganges, and to live surrounded by ghosts in the cremation ground. Bāṇabhaṭṭa's *Kādambarī* (seventh century A.D.) describes the worship of Caṇḍī (a popular name of the goddess Durgā, but also applied sometimes to Kālī) by Śabaras, a tribe of primitive hunters. The worship takes place in the depths of the forest, and blood flows freely.[20] In Vākpati's *Gauḍavaho* (a Prakrit work of the late seventh or early eighth century A.D.) Kālī is described as a non-Aryan goddess, as an aspect of the goddess Vindhyavāsinī (she who dwells in the Vindhya Mountains). She is worshiped by Śabaras, is offered human sacrifices, and is clothed in leaves.[21]

In Bhavabhūti's *Mālatīmādhava* (late seventh or early eighth century A.D.) the heroine, Mālatī, is captured by a female devotee of Cāmuṇḍā, Kapālakuṇḍalā, who intends to sacrifice her to the goddess. Cāmuṇḍā's temple is near a cremation ground. In a hymn of praise to the terrible goddess she is described as dancing wildly and making the worlds shake. She is said to have a gaping mouth, to wear a garland of skulls that laugh and terrify the worlds, to be covered with snakes, to shower flames from her eyes that destroy the worlds, and to be surrounded by fiends and goblins.[22] As in those references mentioned above, Kālī, or Cāmuṇḍā as she is called here, is primarily a terrifying, demonic creature worshiped by those on the periphery of society.[23] She is not identified with the mainstream of Hindu religion, nor does

[19]In at least one Purāṇic account it is Kālī, not Durgā, who slays Śumbha and Niśumbha: *Devī-bhāgavata* V. 30.

[20]Dasgupta, *Bhārater Śakti-sādhana o Śākta Sāhitya*, pp. 66–67.

[21]Verses 285–347; D. C. Sircar, *The Śākta Pīthas* (Delhi: Motilal Banarsidass, n.d.), p. 20; Mazumdar, "Durga," p. 357.

[22]*Bhavabhūti's Mālatīmādhava with the Commentary of Jagaddhara*, ed. and trans. M. R. Kāle, 3d ed. (Delhi: Motilal Banarsidass, 1967), pp. 44–48.

[23]It is significant to note that in the *Mānasāra-śilpaśāstra* (sixth to eighth centuries A.D.) it is said that Kālī's temples should be built far from villages and towns, near the cremation grounds and the dwellings of the Caṇḍālas (9. 289).

she appear as a great goddess in her own right. In this drama, however, there is an early indication of things to come, an indication of Kālī's growing importance in the tradition. For in this drama, despite her terrifying and primarily negative role, she is said to have an important partner in her mad dances: the great dancing god, Śiva himself.[24]

Kālī's Regional Distribution

The view of Kālī as primarily a "peripheral," "negative" goddess is largely borne out in vernacular literature also. A brief look at selected vernacular literature and other data bearing on regional histories discloses something else about Kālī: she is known in several widely separated areas of India, and in several of these areas at quite an early date.

In Tamilnad, Kālī or goddesses very much like her were worshiped from very early times. In the Tamil epic *Śilappadikāram* (traditionally dated as second century B.C. but probably not written until the fourth or fifth century A.D.) the heroine Kaṇṇaki finds herself wandering in the wilderness, where she comes upon a temple of Kālī's. Kālī is called the goddess of death and is said to aid bandits living in the area by bringing them victory in return for their bloody sacrifices.[25] Kaṇṇaki next wanders into a village of tribal hunters, the Eiynars, who are said to raid herding settlements and to plunder travelers. They worship Aiyai, the goddess of hunters, who is described as riding a stag, as decked with snakes, a necklace of tiger's teeth, and a skirt of leopard skin, and as armed with a bow. She is said to receive blood sacrifices, to destroy all with her sword, to be dark in color, and to accept the blood that flows from her devotees' severed heads.[26] In

[24] *Bhavabhūti's Mālatīmādhava*, p. 47.

[25] Prince Ilango Adigal, *Shilappadikaram* ("The Anklet Bracelet"), trans. Alain Danielou (New York: New Directions Book, 1965), canto 11, p. 76.

[26] Ibid., canto 12, pp. 76–85.

the *Maṇimēkalai,* another ancient Tamil epic, a goddess of the forest called the Dark Mother (Karitāy) is described as feeding demons from her beggar's bowl. Her temple is next to the cremation ground.[27] The *Maṇimēkalai* (VI. 50–53) also mentions a temple of Durgā's in which there is a sacrificial altar surrounded by posts with severed heads hanging from them.[28] Pallava and early Cola iconography (fourth to ninth centuries A.D.) indicates that the practice of offering a goddess flesh from nine parts of the body *(navakaṇḍam)* was practiced in the South, as was the offering of one's head.[29] In later times this practice is particularly associated with Kālī.[30] Kālī also appears in later Tamil literature and is known widely in Tamilnad as a village goddess (see below).

Not surprisingly, Kālī figures prominently in Bengali literature, but not until a fairly late date. In the *Maṅgal-kāvyas*, which span several centuries (fifteenth through eighteenth centuries A.D., but reflecting much older indigenous materials) and give the clearest picture of indigenous Bengali religion, for example, Kālī is overshadowed by such goddesses as Manasā, the snake goddess, Sītalā, the goddess of smallpox, and Caṇḍī, a goddess who is associated with the jungles, is the protectress of animals, and is worshiped by hunters.[31] Caṇḍī, of course, is one of the

[27]T. V. Mahalingam, "The Cult of Śakti in Tamilnad," in D. C. Sircar, ed., *The Śakti Cult and Tārā* (Calcutta: University of Calcutta, 1967), p. 20.

[28]Ibid., p. 27.

[29]Ibid.

[30]See, for example, the story of Vīravara, a *kṣatriya* who offers his head to a goddess called variously Caṇḍi, Kālī, and Durgā, and the story of "The Lady Who Caused Her Brother and Husband to Change Heads," in which the heroine sacrifices her head to Durgā, who is described as awful (Somadeva, *The Ocean of Story*, ed. N. M. Penzer, trans. C. H. Tawney, 10 vols. [Delhi: Motilal Banarsidass, 1968], 6:164–207). For human sacrifice to Kālī in Assam, see Edward Gait, *A History of Assam*, 3d rev. ed. (Calcutta: Thacker Spink & Co., 1963), pp. 43, 287–88.

[31]For the *Maṅgal-kāvya* literature see: Asit Kumar Banerjee, *Bangla Sāhityar Itibritta* (Bengali) (Calcutta: Modern Book Agency, 1962), 2: chap 2: "Maṅgal Kāvyer Svarup"; Dinesh Chandra Sen, *History of Bengali Language and Literature*

most famous names of the Goddess in Bengal and India as a whole, and this eventually becomes one of Kālī's epithets. In the various *Caṇḍī-maṅgal-kāvyas* (there being several versions of most *Maṅgal-kāvyas* by different authors writing at different times), however, it is usually clear that the goddess Caṇḍī who appears in the story is not Kālī. She is not terrible in appearance or deed and bears little resemblance to Kālī as she is usually described. Caṇḍī does appear in terrible form on occasion (as in the second episode of the *Caṇḍī-maṅgal-kāvya* concerning Dhanapati Sadagar, a merchant whose son is saved by Caṇḍī in her terrible manifestation), but her appearance is sufficiently different from Kālī's so that it is clear that Kālī herself is not being described. Only in some later versions of the *Annadā-maṅgal-kāvya* (sometimes called the *Kālikā-maṅgal-kāvya*) is Kālī clearly manifested. In the late version of this story by the poet Bhāratcandra Rāy (1712–60), for example, Kālī makes a dramatic appearance when the hero, Sundar, is about to be executed and calls on the goddess for help. She comes to his rescue with an army of demons and ghouls and is described in familiar terms.

> And amidst them all, the goddess—her long and matted hair flowing wildly, she laughed her long and maddened laughter, her third eye scarlet, moving like a disk in her head, her greedy tongue protruding long and loose; she shone with brightness more vertigenous than the sun or fire; she ground her huge hard teeth, her lips drawn back, and streams of blood ran down from her lips' sides; corpses of children swung as earrings from her ears, and on her breast there hung a string of severed heads, with wild and awful faces. Her garland was the intestine of the demon, her girdle one of demons, her ornaments of bones. In lust for blood and flesh the jackals circled round her, and

---

(Calcutta: University of Calcutta, 1954); and T. W. Clark, "Evolution of Hinduism in Medieval Bengali Literature: Śiva, Caṇḍī, Manasā," *Bulletin of the School of Oriental and African Studies* (University of London) 17 (1955): 503–18. Edward Dimock has translated or summarized the *Manasā-maṅgal-kāvya* and the Vidyā-Sundar episode of the *Annadā-maṅgal-kāvya* in *The Thief of Love: Bengali Tales from Court and Village* (Chicago: University of Chicago Press, 1963).

the earth trembled with their howling. She trampled heaven, earth, and hell, crushed them beneath her feet . . . ; her feet were on the breast of prostrate Śiva, lying in meditation-trance with closed eyes.[32]

Although there are a few scattered references to her in early Vaiṣṇava literature,[33] it is only in the eighteenth century that Kālī seems to gain prominence in Bengali vernacular literature, particularly Śākta devotional literature, which will be discussed later.

Archaeological and historical data also do not provide evidence that Kālī was known much earlier. Certain Bengali rulers include her name on their coins (notably Ratnamāṇikya II and Durgāmāṇikya, both of Tripura), but not before the seventeenth century.[34] The public worship of Kālī, which is widespread in Bengal today, does not seem to predate the seventeenth century. The oldest reference to such worship, apparently, is in the *Śyāmāsaparyāvidhi* of Kāśīnātha (seventeenth century).[35] In the eighteenth century two kings of Nadia, Mahārāja Kṛṣṇacandra and his grandson Iśānacandra, formally encouraged such worship. Kṛṣṇacandra commanded that his subjects worship the goddess

[32]Dimock, ed. and trans., *The Thief of Love*, pp. 128–29.

[33]One of the earliest references to Kālī that I have found in Bengal is in Jayānanda's *Caitanya-maṅgala* (a Vaiṣṇava work), which is dated around A.D. 1550. She appears to Jalāl-ud-dīn Fātih Shāh, ruler of Bengal at Navadvip, 1481–87, and terrifies him when he oppresses the *brāhmans*. Kālī's appearance, Jayānanda tells us, halted the ruler's oppression of the Hindus (Jayānanda, *Caitanya-maṅgala*, ed. Nāgendra Nāth Basu [Calcutta: Bangīya Sāhitya Pariṣad, 1905], p. 11; cited in Joseph Thomas O'Connell, "Social Implications of the Gaudīya Vaiṣṇava Movement" [Ph.D. diss., Harvard University, Cambridge, Mass., 1970], p. 102). This reference is significant not only because it is possibly the earliest that we have but also because it allies Kālī with established Hinduism. She protects the *brāhmans* and as such appears as the defender of the faith, as it were.

[34]Bela Lahiri, "Śakti Cult and Coins in North-Eastern India," in Sircar, ed., *The Śakti Cult and Tārā*, p. 37.

[35]Chintaharan Chakravarti, *Tantras: Studies on Their Religion and Literature* (Calcutta: Punthi Pustak, 1963), p. 92.

on threat of punishment, while Iśānacandra celebrated her worship extravagantly.[36] The most popular Tantric works of Bengal that celebrate and describe Kālī are also late. The *Tantrasāra* of Kṛṣṇānanda Agamavāgīśa and the *Śyāmārahasya* of Pūrṇānanda, both of which extol Kālī, are no earlier than the eighteenth century, and Kṛṣṇānanda is sometimes said to be the one who in fact introduced to Bengal the image of Dakṣiṇa-kālī (her most popular image).[37] While the evidence is not conclusive, it would seem that in Bengal, where she is most popular today, Kālī was not widely known or worshiped until a fairly late period.[38]

Kālī is known in other parts of India besides Tamilnad and Bengal, and in some of these areas at a fairly early period. In Assam,[39] Orissa,[40] the Vindhya Mountains region, and western India, particularly Rajasthan, there are temples in her honor and icons of her on a fairly wide scale dating back (in western India) to the fifth century A.D. An interesting point about Kālī in Rajasthan is that she is rarely associated with Durgā, and her worship

[36]Ibid.

[37]Ibid., p. 89.

[38]It is tempting to go further and conclude that Kālī was not indigenous to Bengal but was introduced to Bengal sometime around the sixteenth or seventeenth century. In the *Maṅgal-kāvyas* there is a very clear theme, that of the various goddesses (Caṇḍī, Sītalā, and Manasā) bullying their devotees into worshiping them. This has been interpreted by most scholars as a veiled allusion to Bengali indigenous deities making their way into the Hindu pantheon. This theme is especially clear in the *Manasā-maṅgal-kāvya*, where the hero, Cāndo, a worshiper of Śiva's, is forced into submission by Manasā. Kālī, however, is not cast in this role in Bengali literature, to my knowledge, even when she does appear in certain versions of the *Annadā-maṅgal-kāvya*. My reluctance to insist upon this interpretation, however, stems from the obvious popularity of Kālī in Bengal, both as a "great" goddess and as a village goddess.

[39]Gait, *A History of Assam*.

[40]K. S. Behara, "The Evolution of Śakti Cult at Jajpur, Bhubaneswar and Puri," in Sircar, ed., *The Śakti Cult and Tārā*, pp. 79–86.

(along with Śākta worship generally) declines in the medieval period (when it begins to manifest itself in Bengal).[41]

Some things are clear from this. First, it is evident that Kālī (or goddesses very much like her) was known in, or associated with, several geographically disparate areas of India—the Vindhya Mountains (south-central India), Tamilnad, Bengal, Assam, Orissa, and Rajasthan—thus making it extremely difficult to identify her with any one region or local, indigenous culture. Second, in both Sanskrit and vernacular literature, in both the *Purāṇas* and dramatic literature, Kālī is considered primarily an inauspicious goddess. Although the author of the *Devīmāhātmya* tried to incorporate Kālī into the ranks of Hindu deity by associating her with Durgā, or the Great Goddess (Mahādevī) generally, she was not accepted immediately or unanimously by the tradition. For some time (it is not clear how long or by how many) she was seen primarily as a demonic shrew, worshiped by thieves or by cults and peoples outside, or on the periphery of, Hindu society.

Kālī's Association with Śiva

Kālī did not remain on the periphery of the Hindu tradition, however. In various ways she made her way into the Hindu pantheon and eventually became a popular goddess recognized throughout India. An important means through which this was accomplished, as suggested earlier, was her association with Śiva.

At some point, at least as early as the eighth century A.D. (because she appears with Śiva in Bhavabhūti's *Mālatīmādhava*),

[41]For Kālī in western India and Rajasthan, see D. C. Sircar, "Śakti Cult in Western India," and P. K. Majumdar, "Śakti Worship in Rājasthān," both in Sircar, ed., *The Śakti Cult and Tārā*.

Kālī (and Durgā as well) began to be associated with Śiva.[42] Why this came about is largely a matter of conjecture. Perhaps the tradition recognized in Kālī and certain of the wilder manifestations of Śiva kindred spirits and so gradually came to associate the two, for Śiva, like Kālī, is also a somewhat peripheral deity who dwells in cremation grounds and haunts the wilderness and mountains. Whatever the prime motive in this association, it seems to have taken place fairly early and in a variety of ways.

The *Vāmana-purāṇa* associates the two by making the name "Kālī" (the dark one) one of Pārvatī's epithets. In the long account of Śiva and Pārvatī's wedding (*Vāmana* 25–27) the names Pārvatī and Kālī are used interchangeably. The goddess's appearance, though, has nothing to do with the terrible creature born of Durgā's fury in the *Devī-māhātmya.* The only common feature is her dark complexion, and it is precisely this dark complexion that Pārvatī subsequently rids herself of. (She is embarrassed by it and determines to change it when Śiva jokingly calls her Kālī, a reference to, or slur upon, her dark complexion.) The dark complexion itself, Pārvatī's outward sheath *(koṣa)*, then, takes on an identity of its own in the goddess Kauśikī (she of the sheath), which is one of the most popular names of the

[42]In the *Devī-māhātmya* it is quite clear that Durgā is an independent deity, great in her own right, and only loosely affiliated with any of the great male deities. And if any one of the great gods can be said to be her closest associate, it is Viṣṇu rather than Śiva. It is from Viṣṇu that she is born in the first episode of the *Devī-māhātmya* (81. 68–69). Nowhere in this episode is she associated with Śiva. The same is true of subsequent episodes. When Śiva does appear in the second episode, he is simply one among many male gods who contribute their powers to the creation of Durgā (82. 12–13). In the third episode, in which Kālī is born, the Goddess appears in the form of Pārvatī, emerges from the body of Pārvatī, and proceeds to battle. Now, while it is clear that Pārvatī has been associated with Śiva since at least the time of the *Mahābhārata,* in this myth she appears to be independent of him. Indeed, when Śiva does make an appearance, he is treated as a mere messenger of the Goddess and plays a very minor role in the combat (88. 22–26). It is important to note, too, that Pārvatī appears only after the gods have gone to the Himalayas and petitioned in unison to the "Goddess who is named Viṣṇu-māyā" (85. 6).

goddess in this version of the myth of the slaying of Caṇḍa and Muṇḍa. Kālī as she is known to the *Devī-māhātmya*, the terrible, bloodthirsty ogress, is subsequently born from Kauśikī and defeats Caṇḍa, Muṇḍa, and Raktabīja as in the *Devī-māhātmya.*

The central mythological deeds of Kālī have been changed very little in the *Vāmana-purāṇa.* Kālī is still born from Durgā's wrath at the approach of Caṇḍa and Muṇḍa, and she is described as having a frightful face, a skull-topped staff, a mighty sword, a garland of skulls, and emaciated flesh covered with blood (29. 56—57). She slays Caṇḍa and Muṇḍa at Durgā's command and later is called upon to rescue Durgā when Raktabīja appears to be winning the battle (30). However, the prelude to the great battle against Caṇḍa and Muṇḍa, Pārvatī's marriage to Śiva, clearly shows that Kālī has been associated in name, if not in form, with Śiva's consort. Pārvatī is repeatedly called Kālī, and it is from Pārvatī-Kālī's black skin that Durgā is born, who in turn gives birth to the Kālī of the terrible appearance. To some extent, of course, the version of the Goddess's victory over Caṇḍa and Muṇḍa in the *Vāmana-purāṇa* may be understood as an artificial attempt on the part of the author to relate various strands of the Goddess in order to show that they are all aspects of the one Mahādevī. Be that as it may, in subsequent Hindu history Kālī in fact does become associated with Śiva as his consort-*śakti*, so that when she is shown with a male god it is almost invariably Śiva.

Kālī is associated with Śiva in the same way and in the same story in the *Śiva-purāṇa* (Vāyavīyasaṁhitā I. 24–25). Elsewhere in this *Purāṇa* (which is probably quite late), however, Kālī's association with Śiva is more definitely established. In several places she is part of his retinue of warriors (Rudrasaṁhitā II. 23. 11–12; V. 33. 36–44). When the myths of the *Devī-māhātmya* are retold in condensed form (Umāsaṁhitā 45–49) it is made clear in the text that all goddesses are manifestations of Umā-Satī-Pārvatī, Śiva's spouse. Kālī herself is barely mentioned in this retelling of Durgā's conquest of various demons (although her name appears occasionally as one of Durgā's epithets), but she appears elsewhere as Śiva's helper and in one place is specifically said to have been created from Śiva's hair (Rudra-samhitā II. 32. 25). Thus, in this text it seems that Kālī definitely has become affiliated with Śiva (as his own creation) or with his spouse (as one of her many manifestations).

In the *Liṅga-purāṇa* (II. 100) Kālī's association with Pārvatī (and by implication with Śiva) is firmly and dramatically affirmed by the following myth. Once upon a time the demoness Dārukā obtained such power through asceticism that she usurped the gods and began to rule the world. None of the gods wished to fight a woman, so they all went to Śiva to ask what they should do. He in turn asked Pārvatī if she could save the day for the gods. Hearing her husband's request, Pārvatī created from herself Kālī, with matted hair, three eyes, black skin, a terrible appearance, and a trident and skull. Seeing the terrible goddess, the gods fled in panic, but Kālī, at Pārvatī's command, set out with a band of ghosts and other strange creatures to defeat Dārukā, thus saving the world for the gods. After the battle, in a curious scene, Śiva appears as an infant in the battlefield amidst the corpses of the slain. Seeing him crying there, Kālī picks him up and nurses him. When this does not calm him she begins to dance among the dead with her entourage of ghosts until he becomes delighted and calm.[43] In this text, then, Kālī is clearly associated with Pārvatī, and even plays a positive, motherly role vis-à-vis Śiva.

Kālī and Śiva dance together elsewhere, in different and various contexts. As has been mentioned, they dance together in Kapālakuṇḍalā's hymn in Bhavabhūti's *Mālatīmādhava*. The scene that Kapālakuṇḍalā describes is wild, tumultuous, and world-

[43]The story is summarized in Vans Kennedy, *Researches into the Nature and Affinity of Ancient and Hindu Mythology* (London: Longman, Rees, Orme, Brown & Green, 1831), pp. 337–38.

shaking. Kālī and Śiva appear as mad partners in a cosmic dance that is destined to destroy the worlds. Pārvatī stands by and watches, terrified, and must be comforted by Śiva.

In South India there is a tradition of a dance contest between the two. In every case Śiva is victorious. The context of the tournament differs. In one case it is arranged to settle a debate about the superiority of the sexes. Pārvatī takes the form of Kālī but is still not able to defeat Śiva when he does his Urdhava Tāṇḍava, a particularly strenuous step.[44] In another account of the tournament, Kālī has just slain the demons Śumbha and Niśumbha and becomes intoxicated by drinking their blood. She begins to create havoc and threatens the world itself. Śiva is summoned to save the situation. He assumes his terrible form as Bhairava and appears before the mad goddess. She threatens to kill him but finally agrees to a dance tournament, in which she is eventually defeated and pacified.[45] The same story is told by Śivaprakasar in the *Tirukkūvappurāṇam*,[46] but here the scene takes place after Kālī has defeated Dārukā (as in the *Liṅga-purāṇa*). Finally, there is a story concerning the origin of the Cidambaram temple, a famous South Indian Śaivite holy place. In this temple legend it is said that the site originally belonged to, or was guarded by, Kālī. When some Śaivite devotees sought to have a vision of Śiva there, she drove them away, whereupon Śiva appeared, challenged her to a dance tournament, and defeated her.[47]

There are some obvious conclusions that can be drawn from these South Indian stories of Śiva's defeat of Kālī in a dance

[44] *Tirupputtūrp-purāṇam, Daruka vaṇa-c*, 115th *carukkam;* cited in M. A. Dorai Rangaswamy, *The Religion and Philosophy of Tēvāram* (Madras: University of Madras, 1958), book 1, p. 442.

[45] *Tiruvālaṅkāṭṭu-p purāṇam;* cited in ibid., p. 444.

[46] Cited in ibid., p. 445.

[47] R. K. Das, *Temples of Tamilnad* (Bombay: Bharatiya Vidya Bhavan, 1964), p. 195.

contest. The stories probably reflect the Śaivite confrontation with and accommodation of Kālī, and perhaps an indigenous goddess cult. Since Kālī is still worshiped as a village deity in South India[48] and has there the characteristics of a "deity of the place,"[49] it is likely that she, or a goddess (or goddesses) like her, was indigenous to the South. The contest, then, may mark the Śaivite accommodation of a "little tradition" as well as the accommodation of a growing, all-India Kālī mythology and cult. In these stories, moreover, it is clear that Kālī is subdued by Śiva. She is not accepted on equal terms. All of the stories smack of the Śaivite point of view. The best that Kālī can hope for is marriage with Śiva, never conquest or domination of him.[50]

There are some other, more specifically religious, implications to be drawn from the story of the dance tournament. Māṇikka Vāchakar, for example, says that had Śiva not defeated or calmed Kālī, the whole universe would have become subject to her blind, bubbling fury and destroyed itself. Her fury is equated with *prakṛti*—the realm of vibrating matter that proceeds according to its own laws. Śiva by subduing Kālī represents Puruṣa, or the *yogin's* heroic taming of matter; his defeat of Kālī is "a sublimation and deification of matter."[51]

There are other stories, usually in later literature, that depict the confrontation and association of Kālī and Śiva in such a way as to give Kālī the dominant position in their relationship. A striking instance of this is to be found (not surprisingly) in the *Devī-bhāgavata.* Once upon a time, the story goes, all of heaven's inhabitants were invited to Dakṣa's sacrifice with the exception

[48]Henry Whitehead, *The Village Gods of South India* (Calcutta: Association Press, 1921).

[49]See Kees W. Bolle, "Speaking of a Place," in Joseph M. Kitagawa and Charles H. Long, eds., *Myths and Symbols: Studies in Honor of Mircea Eliade* (Chicago: University of Chicago Press, 1969), pp. 127–39.

[50]Rangaswamy, *The Religion of Tēvāram*, book 1, p. 490.

[51]Ibid., p. 491.

of Śiva. Dakṣa thought Śiva was a bit mad and really unfit to be his daughter's (Satī's) husband, so he did not invite him. Satī, nevertheless, did not want to miss this important social event, so she asked Śiva if she might attend, even though he had not been invited. Śiva refused permission, and in anger Satī assumed the terrible form of Kālī. Śiva, terrified of this awful creature, tried to flee, whereupon Kālī filled the ten directions with her various (and mostly terrible) forms.[52] Śiva, unable to escape, sat down and in great fear looked at Kālī and asked who she was and where his lovely Satī had gone. She replied that of course she *was* his beloved Satī, only this was her real form, the form she assumed for the tasks of creation and destruction. It was her form as universal deity. She explained to Śiva that she had assumed the beautiful form of Satī simply to reward Śiva for his austerities.[53]

Another story that pictures Kālī dominating Śiva is set in the context of the *Rāmāyaṇa*. When Rāma returns from Laṅkā he brags to Sītā about his conquest of the terrible ten-headed Rāvaṇa. Sītā, however, is not impressed and simply smiles. When Rāma's boasting continues, Sītā asks him what he would do if he were to confront a thousand-headed Rāvaṇa. Rāma replies that, of course, he would slay such a Rāvaṇa. Sītā looks doubtful and says that in fact such a demon does exist but that he had better let *her* confront him. Rāma, indignant, sets out

[52]This myth is very common in later literature and tells of the origin of the *daśa-mahāvidyās,* the ten great forms or manifestations of the Devī. While Kālī is said to be the source of all the forms in this particular myth, she is usually said to be the first of the ten forms. See Sircar, *The Śākta Pithas*, p. 48 n.

[53]Summarized in Arthur Avalon, ed., *Principles of Tantra: The Tantratattva of Śrīyukta Śiva Candra Vidyārnava Bhattacārya Mahodaya* (Madras: Ganesh & Co., 1960), pp. 208–13. Kālī's rewarding of Śiva for his austerities by condescending to become his wife (in the form of Satī) is a reversal of their courtship as told in most other texts. In most versions Pārvatī wins Śiva's grace through her austerities. The reversal of roles in this myth effectively subordinates Śiva to his consort.

with his army to find the new terror. Finding the thousand-headed Rāvaṇa, Rāma and his army attack. However, when the giant sees the approaching army he shoots just three arrows, which drive all of Rāma's allies back to their homes. Alone on the battlefield with the giant Rāvaṇa, Rāma is disheartened and begins to weep. Sītā, seeing the predicament of her husband, smiles and immediately assumes the form of Kālī. She attacks and kills the demon; then she begins tossing his heads and limbs about. She gulps his blood in her frenzy and begins to do an earth-shattering dance. The gods become alarmed and petition Śiva to intervene. He comes to the battlefield where Kālī is dancing in madness and throws himself down among the corpses of the slain under her dancing feet. Brahmā then calls to her, directing her attention to Śiva beneath her. Recognizing him (he is called her husband here) she is astonished and embarrassed and stops her dance. (This is a very common representation of Kālī in Bengal.) She resumes her appearance as Sītā and accompanies the humiliated Rāma to their home.[54]

This myth presents us with a very different picture of Kālī's association with Śiva. Here she dominates the action. Śiva is summoned to remedy the situation, to be sure, but he can do so only by lying beneath her feet. He subdues her, certainly, but only by humiliating himself. Here, clearly, Kālī has triumphed over Śiva—she has moved to the foreground as the more powerful of the two. And this dominant position is to be seen elsewhere: in certain Tantric literature and in Bengali Śākta devotionalism.

[54]The myth is told in W. Ward, *A View of the History, Literature, and Religion of the Hindoos,* 3d ed., abr. (London: Black, Parbury & Allen, 1817), pp. 146–47. Ward may be mistaken in attributing this story to the *Adhyātma Rāmāyaṇa*, however. Sir Monier Monier-Williams alludes to the same myth and says that it is found in the *Adbhuta Rāmāyaṇa* (*Brahmanism and Hinduism,* 3d ed. [London: John Murray, 1887], pp. 189–90 n.).

Chapter III

Kālī and the Tantric Hero

It was suggested above that among the three most important factors bringing about Kālī's "completion" as a great deity in her own right was her popularity in Tantrism. Coincident with the rise of Tantrism was the increasing popularity of the feminine in the Indian tradition. While goddesses were known and worshiped in Hinduism prior to the Tantric "epidemic," it was in the early medieval period (from the seventh century A.D. onward) that the Goddess (or goddesses) assumed a new popularity, far more overwhelming than anything in the past. To what extent Tantrism encouraged, reinforced, or even presupposed the emergence of the Goddess is difficult to determine. That the increasing importance of the feminine blended well with certain Tantric emphases, however, is quite clear,[55] for an essential aspect of Tantrism (both Hindu and Buddhist) is the interplay, union, and symbiotic relationship of the male and female aspects of reality (Śiva and Śakti in Hinduism, Upāya and Prajña in Buddhism). Just when and how Kālī became accepted into the Tantric tradition is obscure.[56] By late medieval times (sixteenth century), though, she was intimately associated with Tantrism, particularly Tantrism of the left-handed, esoteric tradition, or that aspect of the Tantric tradition that emphasized the path of the hero *(vīra)*.[57]

[55]Debiprasad Chattopadhyaya relates Tantrism to indigenous, agricultural cultures that had matriarchal kinship systems and were essentially opposed to Aryan, brāhmanic religion (*Lokāyata: A Study in Ancient Indian Materialism* [New Delhi: People's Publishing House, 1959]).

[56]The Hindu *Tantras* are usually set in the context of divine revelation (or divine discourse) in which Śiva instructs Pārvatī or in which Pārvatī is the teacher. Never, to my knowledge, does Kālī play either role. Pārvatī alone seems to play the role of disciple or teacher.

[57]The Vāmācāra, in which Kālī comes to play an important, if not central, role, seems to have been most popular in Bengal and Assam, those areas where she is still most widely worshiped, and this may suggest that Kālī originally came from

In many Tantric texts Kālī's position is unambiguously declared to be that of a great deity; indeed, in many texts she is declared the supreme deity, triumphant over all others, equivalent, in fact, to Brahman. In the *Nirvāṇa-tantra* the great gods Brahmā, Viṣṇu, and Śiva are said to arise from her like bubbles from the sea, endlessly arising and passing away, leaving their source unchanged. Compared to Kālī, this text proclaims, the gods Brahmā, Viṣṇu, and Śiva are like the amount of water in a cow's hoofprint compared to the waters of the sea.[58] The *Nigama-kalpataru* and the *Picchilā-tantra* declare that of all *mantras* Kālī's is the greatest.[59] The *Yoginī-tantra,* the *Kāmākhyā-tantra,* and the *Niruttara-tantra* all proclaim Kālī the greatest of the *vidyās* (the manifestations of the Goddess), or divinity itself; indeed, they declare her to be the essence or own form *(svarūpa)* of the Goddess.[60] The *Kāmadā-tantra* states unequivocally that she is attributeless, neither male nor female, sinless, the imperishable *saccidānanda* (being, consciousness, and bliss), Brahman itself.[61] In the *Mahānirvāṇa-tantra,* too, "Kālī" is one of the most common epithets for the primordial Śakti,[62] and in one passage Śiva praises her as follows:

> At the dissolution of things, it is Kāla [Time] Who will devour all, and by reason of this He is called Mahākāla [an epithet of Śiva], and since Thou devourest Mahākāla Himself, it is Thou who art the Supreme Primordial Kālikā.

---

the northeastern area of India. However, her place as a village deity in South India, her association with the Vindhya Mountains and western India, and her relatively late appearance in Bengali literature suggest that she was probably not indigenous to Bengal alone.

[58] Avalon, ed., *Principles of Tantra,* pp. 327–28.

[59] *Hymn to Kālī (Karpūrādi-stotra)*, ed. and trans. Arthur Avalon [John Woodroffe], 3d ed. (Madras: Ganesh & Co., 1965), p. 34.

[60] Ibid.

[61] Ibid.

[62] *E.g.*, V. 140–41; VI. 68–76; X. 102.

Because Thou devourest Kāla, Thou art Kalī, because Thou art the Origin of and devourest all things Thou art called the Adyā [primordial] Kalī. Resuming after dissolution Thine own nature, dark and formless, ineffable and inconceivable Thou alone remainest as the One. Though having a form, yet art Thou formless; though Thyself without beginning, multiform by the power of Māyā, Thou art the Beginning of all, Creatrix, Protectress, and Destructress that Thou art.[63]

Why and how Kālī came to be associated with Tantrism are not clear, nor is it clear how she came to gain such a preeminent position. Given certain Tantric philosophical and ritual presuppositions, however, the following line of argument seems quite probable.

Tantrism generally is ritually oriented. By means of various rituals (exterior and interior, bodily and mental) the *sādhaka* (practitioner) seeks to gain *mokṣa* (release, salvation). A consistent theme in this endeavor is the uniting of opposites (male-female, microcosm-macrocosm, sacred-profane, Śiva-Śakti). In Tantrism there is an elaborate, subtle geography of the body that must be learned, controlled, and ultimately resolved in unity. By means of the body—both the physical and the subtle bodies—the *sādhaka* may manipulate various levels of reality and harness the dynamics of those levels to the attainment of his goal. The *sādhaka*, with the help of a *guru*, undertakes to gain his goal by conquest, by using his own body and knowledge of that body to bring the fractured world of name and form, the polarized world of male and female, sacred and profane, to wholeness and unity.

In Vāmācāra *sādhana* (spiritual endeavor) this quest takes a particularly dramatic form. In his attempt to realize the nature of the world as completely and thoroughly pervaded by the one Śakti, the *sādhaka* (here called the hero, *vīra*) undertakes the ritual known as *pañca-tattva*, the ritual of the five ("forbidden")

[63]*Mahānirvāṇa-tantra* IV. 29–34; *The Great Liberation (Mahānirvāna Tantra)*, trans. Arthur Avalon [John Woodroffe], 4th ed. (Madras: Ganesh & Co., 1963), pp. 69–70.

things (or truths). In a ritual context and under the supervision of his *guru*, the *sādhaka* partakes of wine, meat, fish, parched grain, and sexual intercourse. In this way he overcomes the distinction (or duality) of clean and unclean, sacred and profane, and breaks his bondage to a world artificially fragmented. He affirms in a radical way the underlying unity of the phenomenal world, the identity of Śakti with the whole creation. Heroically, he triumphs over it, controls and masters it. By affirming the essential worth of the forbidden, he causes the forbidden to lose its power to pollute, to degrade, to bind.[64]

The figure of Kālī conveys the image of death, destruction, fear, terror, the all-consuming aspect of reality. As such she is also a "forbidden thing," or the forbidden par excellence, for she is death itself. For the Tantric hero the forbidden is not to be propitiated, feared, ignored, or avoided. Given the rationale of the *pañca-tattva* ritual, Kālī is confronted boldly by the *sādhaka* and thereby assimilated, overcome, and transformed into a vehicle of salvation. This is particularly clear in the *Karpūrādi-stotra,* a short work in praise of Kālī, which describes the *pañca-tattva* ritual as performed in the cremation ground *(śmaśāna-sādhana)*. Throughout this text Kālī is described in familiar terms. She is black (verse 1), she has disheveled hair, blood trickles from her mouth (verse 3), she holds a sword and a severed head (verse 4), she wears a girdle of severed arms, she sits on a corpse in the cremation ground (verse 7), and she is surrounded by skulls, bones, and female jackals (verse 8). It is she, when confronted boldly in meditation, who gives the *sādhaka* great power and ultimately salvation. In her favorite dwelling place, the cremation ground, the *sādhaka* with his female companion

[64]For the *pañca-tattva* ritual see *Mahānirvāṇa-tantra* V and VI; Agehananda Bharati, *The Tantric Tradition* (London: Rider & Co., 1965), pp. 228–78; Mircea Eliade, *Yoga: Immortality and Freedom*, trans. Willard Trask (New York: Pantheon Books, 1958), pp. 254–62; and Heinrich Zimmer, *Philosophies of India*, ed. Joseph Campbell (Cleveland: World Publishing Co., 1956), pp. 572–80.

(śakti) meditates on every terrible aspect of the Black Goddess and thus achieves his goal.

He, O Mahākālī, who in the cremation-ground, naked, and with dishevelled hair, intently meditates upon Thee and recites Thy *mantra*, and with each recitation makes offering to Thee of a thousand *Akaṇda* flowers with seed, becomes without any effort a Lord of the earth.
O Kālī, whoever on Tuesday at midnight, having uttered Thy *mantra* makes offering even but once with devotion to Thee of a hair of his *Śakti* in the cremation-ground, becomes a great poet, a Lord of the earth, and even goes mounted upon an elephant.[65]

Here it is clear that Kālī is more than a terrible, ferocious slayer of demons who serves Durgā (or Śiva) on the battlefield. In fact, she is by and large disassociated from the battle context. She is the supreme mistress of the universe (verse 12), she is identified with the five elements (verse 14,), and, in union with Śiva (who is clearly identified as her spouse[66]), she creates and destroys the worlds. Her appearance has also been modified befitting her exalted position as ruler of the world and the object of meditation by which the *sādhaka* attains liberation. In addition to her terrible aspects (which are insisted upon) there are now hints .of

[65]*Karpūrādi-stotra* 15–16 (*Hymn to Kālī,* pp. 84, 86). Cf. the *dhyāna-mantra* of Śmaśana-kālī in Kṛṣṇānanda Āgamavāgīśa's *Tantrasāra* 1:374:

She is dark as soot, always living in the cremation ground. Her eyes are pink, her hair disheveled, her body gaunt and fearful. In her left hand she holds a cup filled with wine and meat, and in her right hand she holds a freshly cut human head. She smiles and eats rotten meat. She is decked with ornaments, is naked, and is absorbed in drinking. Having conceived the deity in this way, one should propitiate her in the cremation ground. The householder will worship her at home, at dead of night having partaken of fish, meat, and wine and being naked.

[66]In at least one Tantric text Kālī is identified with Lakṣmī and by implication Viṣṇu: *Lakṣmī-tantra,* ed. Pandit V. Krishnamacharya (Madras: Adyar Library & Research Centre, 1959), VII. 13. Since this is a Pāñcarātra text, it is hardly surprising that Kālī is identified with Lakṣmī, given the overwhelming Vaiṣṇava bias of this school.

another, benign dimension. So, for example, she is no longer described as emaciated or ugly. In the *Karpūrādi-stotra* she is young and beautiful (verse 1), she has a gently smiling face (verse 18), and her two right hands make gestures that dispel fear and offer boons (verse 4). These positive features are entirely apt, as Kālī no longer is a mere shrew, the distillation of Durgā's wrath, but is she through whom the hero achieves success, she who grants the boon of salvation, and she who, when boldly approached, frees the *sādhaka* from fear itself. She is here not only the symbol of death but the symbol of triumph over death.

In Tantrism Kālī has come to represent the forbidden par excellence, on the one hand, and the bountiful, fear-dispelling, boon-conferring goddess on the other. Through bold confrontation the heroic practitioner finds within the terrifying, forbidden, frightening presence of Kālī the key to his triumph over his own fears.[67] The Tantric hero has refused to flee before the wrath of the goddess and in that refusal has gained mastery over her and over himself.

Kālī and Bengali Devotionalism

The third important factor that was mentioned earlier as central in the history of Kālī's "completion" (or revelation) is Bengali

[67]Perhaps this is how some of the wrathful deities of Tibetan (Tantric) Buddhism are to be understood. The *Bardo Thödol* makes clear, for example, that the fearful deities one confronts after death are merely the creations of one's own mind and should not be feared. They represent one's own actions and subconscious fears and as such are projections of one's inner being that must be mastered. See *The Tibetan Book of the Dead or the After-Death Experiences on the Bardo Plane, According to Lāma Kazi Dawa-Samdup's English Rendering*, ed. W. Y. Evans-Wentz (London: Oxford University Press, 1960), part 2, and Giuseppe Tucci, *Theory and Practice of the Maṇḍala*, trans. A. H. Broderick (New York: Samuel Weiser, 1970), p. 53. The importance of cemeteries as places of meditation is also seen in Tibetan Buddhism, perhaps for the same reason: that is, by confronting death one overcomes one's fear of it. See Tucci, pp. 41–42, and P. H. Pott, *Yoga and Yantra*, trans. Rodney Needham (The Hague: Martinus Nijhoff, 1966), pp. 76–101.

Śākta devotion. This is perhaps the most remarkable episode in Kālī's "affair" with the Hindu tradition, and it reveals clearly her ultimate acceptance by that tradition. This devotion is typified by two of Bengal's most famous religious figures: Rāmprasād Sen and Ramakrishna.

Rāmprasād (1718–75) was of the Vaidya caste and was educated as a physician, although it seems that he never actually practiced this profession. Instead, he took a clerical job for the manager of a large estate. He found his work tedious and spent much of his time scrawling verses in his books. When his employer discovered this preoccupation he released Rāmprasād from his responsibilities and became his patron, providing him with a pension. He was soon introduced to the Kṛṣṇanagar Court and earned the title *kavirañjana,* "entertainer of poets." Most of his life, however, does not seem to have been spent at court. The milieu reflected in his songs is not courtly but rustic. His songs complain of hardship, family troubles, and the deprivations of a "mud hut" peasant. His songs are simple, full of Bengali village imagery, and widely known and loved all over Bengal. Although he was an educated man and even spent some time at the Kṛṣṇanagar Court, he and his songs have entered the bloodstream of Bengali culture and religion. His songs are known and sung by both the illiterate manual laborer and the highly educated Bengali *"babu."* His impact on Bengali religion and the importance of his devotion in the history of Kālī's completion are difficult to overestimate.

The goddess of Rāmprasād's devotional hymns is the one familiar to the Hindu tradition up to his time: the Kālī who is black, ferocious, and terrible to behold, the dweller in the cremation ground, she who reveals (or is) the world process, the entire creation in all its ambiguity. Rāmprasād sees in her the mistress of a mad, reeling world.

O Mother! Thou art present in every form;
Thou art in the entire universe and in its tiniest
and most trifling things.
Wherever I go and wherever I look,
I see Thee, Mother, present in thy cosmic form.
The whole world—earth, water, fire and air—
All are thy forms, O Mother, the whole world of
birth and death.
"Mountains, plants, animals living on land and in
water,
All moving and unmoving beings in this beautiful
world," says Prasāda, "are full of Divine Will."[68]

O Mother! who can understand Thy magic [*māyā*]?
Thou art a mad Goddess; Thou hast made all mad with
attachment.
Under the influence of Thy magic none can recognize
any other in this world.
All imitate others' actions—such is Kālī's wrath!
Such is the agony caused by [such a] mad Goddess
that none can know Her aright.
Rāma Prasāda says, "All sufferings vanish, if She
grants Her grace."[69]

Rāmprasād sees in Kālī the world revealed in all its harsh, indifferent, seemingly capricious aspects, and a constant theme in his poetry is petulant complaint to this "stony-hearted" deity.

Let us have a word or two about the problem of suffering. Let us talk about suffering, Tārā, let me express my mind.

Some say that you are humble and full of kindness.

Yes, Mother, to some you have given wealth, horses, elephants, charioteers, conquest. And the lot of others is field labcur, with rice and vegetables. Some live in palaces, as I myself would like to do. O Mother, are these fortunate folk your grandfathers and I no relation at all?

[68]*Rama Prasada's Devotional Songs: The Cult of Shakti*, trans. Jadunath Sinha (Calcutta: Sinha Publishing House, 1966), no. 6, p. 3.

[69]Ibid., no. 138, p. 75.

Some wear shawls and comfortable wrappers, they have sugar and curds as well as rice.

Some ride in *pālkis* [palanquins], while I have the privilege of carrying them.

Mother, through what grain land of yours have I driven my plough?

Prasād says: If I forget you, I endure the burden of grief that burns. Mother, my desire is to become the dust of those Feet that banish fear.[70]

As in Tantrism, Kālī represents for Rāmprasād the world order, particularly the darker dimensions of reality. But Rāmprasād, unlike the Tantric hero, does not come to terms with Kālī by heroically confronting her, by challenging her manfully. For in his songs Kālī is revealed as "Mother," a caring presence, and the devotee's approach to her is as a helpless, forlorn, but stubborn child.

Ever must I remain thus? Thou who art gracious to the lowly, what is to befall me? I am without deeds, without merit of worship, weak and poor inconceivably. Ah, wilt thou fulfil this my impossible wish? Shall I gain those Feet?

Whether I am an obedient child or disobedient, is not all known to those Feet? Though her child be disobedient, does the mother forsake it? To whom shall I speak all this?

Prasād has said: "Except Tārā's, what other name is there I can take? Śiva has cherished this name in his heart."[71]

I shall take refuge in my Mother's feet; where shall
I go at this time of my distress?
If there is no room for me at Her abode, I will lie
outside; there is no harm in it.

[70]Edward J. Thompson and Arthur Marsham Spencer, trans., *Bengali Religious Lyrics, Śākta* (Calcutta: Association Press, 1923), no. 7, pp. 34–35. Rāmprasād sometimes uses the names Tārā, Durgā, and Kālī interchangeably when addressing the goddess of his affections. For Rāmprasād it is clear that all goddesses are manifestations of one supreme goddess. On the other hand, it is also clear that the form he cherished above all others was Kālī.

[71]Ibid., no. 44, p. 58.

Fasting with Her name as my support, I will lie
outside Her abode.
Prasāda says: "I will not leave Her even if Umā
turns me out;
I will catch hold of Her feet with outstretched arms
and give up my life."[72]

Rāmprasād never forgets Kālī's demonic, frightening aspects. He does not distort Kālī's nature and the truths she reveals; he does not refuse to meditate on her terrifying features. He mentions these repeatedly in his songs but is never put off or repelled by them. Kālī may be frightening, the mad, forgetful, negligent mistress of a world spinning out of control, but she is, after all, the Mother of all. As such, she must be accepted by her children—accepted in wonder and awe, perhaps, but accepted nevertheless.

O Kālī! why dost Thou roam about nude?
Art Thou not ashamed, Mother!
Garb and ornaments Thou hast none; yet Thou
pridest in being King's daughter.
O Mother! is it a virtue of Thy family that Thou
placest thy feet on Thy Husband?
Thou art nude; Thy Husband is nude; you both roam
cremation grounds.
O Mother! we are all ashamed of you; do put on Thy
garb.
Thou has cast away Thy necklace of jewells, Mother,
and worn a garland of human heads.
Prasāda says, "Mother! Thy fierce beauty has frightened
Thy nude Consort."[73]

[72]*Rama Prasada's Devotional Songs*, no. 12, p. 6. The following lines, attributed to Rāmprasād, express this theme concisely: "Though she beat it, the child clings to its mother, crying 'Mother' " (Thompson and Spencer, trans., *Bengali Religious Lyrics, Śākta*, p. 22).

[73]*Rama Prasada's Devotional Songs*, no. 181, p. 97.

In this acceptance, which encompasses Kālī's weird, terrible nature, Rāmprasād, like the Tantric *sādhaka,* wins the boon of overcoming death. In his childlike acceptance of Kālī, in his openness to her and what she represents, he triumphs over death. Through self-surrender *(prapatti)* he loses his fear of the death of self, which is all death really is.

> O Kālī! Thou art fond of cremation grounds; so
> I have turned my heart into one
> That Thou, a resident of cremation grounds, may
> dance there unceasingly.
> O Mother! I have no other fond desire in my
> heart; fire of a funeral pyre is burning there;
> O Mother! I have preserved the ashes of dead bodies
> all around that Thou may come.
> O Mother! keeping Śiva, conqueror of Death, under
> Thy feet,
> Come, dancing to the tune of music; Prasāda waits
> with his eyes closed.[74]

> I am lying at Thy feet, O Mother, Thou dost not
> look at me even once.
> Thou art engrossed in Thy play, O Kālī, Thou art
> immersed in Thy thought.
> What play dost Thou play on earth, in heaven and
> hell?
> All close their eyes in terror and cry "Mother!"
> "Mother!" grasping Thy feet.
> O Mother! Thou has great dissolution in Thy hand;
> Śiva lies at Thy feet, absorbed in bliss.
> Thou laughest aloud (striking terror); streams of
> blood flow from Thy limbs.
> O Tārā, doer of good, the good of all, grantor of
> safety, O Mother, grant me safety.
> O Mother Kālī! take me in Thy arms; O Mother Kālī!
> take me in Thy arms.

[74]Ibid., no. 167, p. 89.

O Mother! come now as Tārā with a smiling face and
clad in white;
As dawn descends on dense darkness of the night.
O Mother! terrific Kālī! I have worshipped Thee
alone so long.
My worship is finished; now, O Mother, bring down
Thy sword.[75]

It is difficult to exaggerate the importance of Rāmprasād in the history of Kālī's worship in Bengal. Before Rāmprasād worship of her seems to have been primarily esoteric, performed in the context of Tantric *sādhana* by individuals or small groups in secret. Beginning with Rāmprasād, however, and primarily as a result of him, her worship became "public."[76] In Rāmprasād a path was revealed that was efficacious and appropriate to the masses of ordinary people. Kālī was strange, terrible, frightening, and clearly mad, but she was, for all that, "Mother." She might be fickle, indifferent, and unpredictable, but if petitioned openly, stubbornly—as a child petitions its mother—she might become the grantor of comfort and peace to her suffering child.

Ramakrishna (1836–86) was born in a small village south of Calcutta. Although his family was *brāhman*, his early environment was simple. His family were peasants, and he himself always remained a naïve, simple peasant at heart. His formal education was limited to the rudiments of reading and writing, and he never learned or spoke any language but Bengali. At sixteen he left his village and went to Calcutta to live with his elder brother, who ran a small school there. He earned his livelihood by acting as a *pūjārī,* offering worship (as a *brāhman*) to images in houses and shops of non-*brāhmans*. When his brother

[75]Ibid., no. 221, pp. 118–19. For Rāmprasād's overcoming of death and the fear of death, see also Thompson and Spencer, trans., *Bengali Religious Lyrics, Śākta*, nos. 42, 54, 57, and 58, pp. 57, 63–64, 65, and 65–66.

[76]Mahārāja Kṛṣṇacandra and Īśānacandra of Nadia may have been influenced by Rāmprasād in their decisions to institute public worship of Kālī. See p. 99.

accepted an invitation to become the temple priest at a newly founded Kālī temple at Dakṣiṇeśvar, on the banks of the Hooghly just north of Calcutta, Ramakrishna followed him and acted as his assistant. A year later his borther died, and Ramakrishna was invited to stay on as the temple priest. In that capacity and at that temple he spent the rest of his life. He gathered about him a small group of devotees, the most famous of whom was Vivekānanda (1863–1902), the founder of the Ramakrishna Mission. As her official temple servant, Ramakrishna pampered and doted upon Mother Kālī for most of his life. In the style of Rāmprasād he approached her as a child, and in his spontaneous, open, and naïve devotion is seen the final episode in Kālī's "taming."

Ramakrishna, like Rāmprasād, did not ignore, but insisted upon, Kālī's wild, bizarre nature. In his biographies he is often described or quoted as marveling at Kālī's extreme appearance and odd behavior.[77] She was for him, as she was for Rāmprasād, the Mistress (but also the Mother) of a dizzying, intoxicated creation. Either in his own words, or in those of Rāmprasād, which he loved and often invoked, he sang of his Mother dancing out the rhythms of the world in frenzy or madness.

> Behold my Mother playing with Shiva, lost in an
>   ecstasy of joy!
> Drunk with a draught of celestial wine, She reels,
>   and yet does not fall.
> Erect She stands on Shiva's bosom, and the earth
>   trembles under Her tread;
> She and Her Lord are mad with frenzy, casting
>   aside all fear and shame![78]

[77]There are two biographical works about Ramakrishna: M. [Mahendranath Gupta], *The Gospel of Sri Ramakrishna*, trans. Swami Nikhilananda (New York: Ramakrishna-Vivekananda Center, 1942), and Swami Saradananda, *Sri Ramakrishna, the Great Master*, trans. Swami Jagadananda (Madras: Sri Ramakrishna Math, 1952).

[78]M., *Gospel of Ramakrishna*, pp. 494–95.

The world is created and destroyed in Kālī's wild dancing, and the truth of redemption lies in man's awareness that he is invited to take part in that dance, to yield to the frenzied beat of the Mother's dance of life and death. Redemption lies in the realization that one is in the hands (or beneath the feet) of Kālī and that ultimately one is directed by the Mother's will.

> O Kali, my Mother full of Bliss! Enchantress of
> the almighty Shiva!
> In Thy delirious joy Thou dancest, clapping Thy
> hands together! . . .
> Thou art the Mover of all that move, and we are
> but Thy helpless toys.[79]

The world is created by Kālī in play and for her amusement. The world—life and particularly individual biographies—delights her. Man, as her plaything, her toy, her puppet, finds fulfillment in joining Kālī's play, in clapping his hands in delight, in giving himself up in self-surrender to her mad escapade. He is redeemed when he lets go of adult pretensions and yields to the Mother's game.

> Master [Ramakrishna]: "The Divine Mother is always playful and sportive. This universe is Her play. She is self-willed and must always have Her own way. She is full of bliss. She gives freedom to one out of a hundred thousand."
>
> A Brahmo Devotee [a member of the Brahmo Samaj, a reform movement founded by Ram Mohan Roy in 1829]: "But sir, if She likes, She can give freedom to all. Why, then, has She kept us bound to the world?"
>
> Master: "That is Her will. She wants to continue playing with Her created beings. In a game of hide-and-seek the running about soon stops if in the beginning all the players touch the 'granny.' If all touch Her, then how can the game go on? That displeases Her. Her pleasure is in continuing the game."[80]

[79]Ibid., p. 223.

[80]Ibid., p. 136.

Man, in the final analysis, however, can influence the Mother, for he, too, has a master-string by means of which he can "control" the Mother's apparent caprice. Through love, through the naïve, steadfast devotion of a child, man can make the Mother dance too—can make her reveal an aspect of herself that is normally kept well hidden. "Prema [devotional love] is the rope by which you can tether God, as it were. Whenever you want to see Him you have merely to pull the rope. Whenever you call Him, He will appear before you."[81]

> O Mother, what a machine is this that Thou has made!
> What pranks Thou playest with this toy
> Three and a half cubits high!
> Hiding Thyself within, Thou holdest the guiding string;
> But the machine, not knowing it,
> Still believes it moves by itself.
> Whoever finds the Mother remains a machine no more;
> Yet some machines have even bound
> The Mother Herself with the string of love.[82]

To a greater degree than even Rāmprasād, Ramakrishna embodied the qualities of a child when he approached Mother Kālī.[83] As her full-time servant at the Dakṣiṇeśvar temple he was divorced from worldly problems and free to devote his entire life to her service. When he approahced Kālī he did so as the child he was, with utter simplicity, wholehearted eagerness, and complete naïveté. He is described by one of his disciples as follows:

> Like a drunkard, he would reel to the throne of the Mother, touch Her chin by way of showing his affection for Her, and sing, talk, joke, laugh, and dance. . . . As his spiritual mood deepened he more

[81]Ibid., p. 502.

[82]Ibid., pp. 193–94.

[83]For Ramakrishna's childlike nature and his own teachings about the childlike nature of true devotees, see Kinsley, "The Divine Player," pp. 314–34.

and more felt himself to be a child of the Divine Mother. He learnt to surrender himself completely to Her will and let her direct him.[84]

And as Ramakrishna was childlike when he approached Kālī, she too became like a child in response to him. Behind her dreadful appearance she finally revealed to Ramakrishna that hidden child. Ramakrishna himself relates a vision he had of her: "She came to me . . . as a (Muslim) girl six or seven years old. She had a tilak on her forehead and was naked. She walked with me, joking and frisking like a child."[85]

In Bengal today Kālī is extremely popular. Her images are found in thousands of temples throughout the country, and on Kālī Pūjā day (her most important festival day and not to be confused with Durgā Pūjā) thousands of additional temporary images are set up in *pandals* throughout the state. In South Calcutta, in the Keoratala-śmaśāna, one of the largest cremation grounds in the city, an immense image of Kālī is set up. Large crowds jam the vicinity and jostle the funeral processions that stream to the burning ground twenty-four hours a day. Shortly after midnight, to the sharp, staccato beat of drums and the shouts of the assembly, "Victory to Kālī, victory to the Mother," several black goats are beheaded and offered to the goddess (as they are every day at the nearby Kālīghat temple). The funeral pyres blaze in the background, and the Black Goddess is served. Kālī retains her fierce appearance and her appetite for blood, clearly. But alongside many of her images on this day, Ramakrishna and his wife are shown sitting placidly. Kālī stands behind them, looking terrible as ever, but her hands are placed gently on their heads. There she stands, lolling tongue, bloodied sword, and all—but comforting her trusting children. She is tamed.

[84]M., *Gospel of Ramakrishna*, pp. 14–15.

[85]Ibid., p. 175.

Chapter III

Summary

Kālī breaks into the Great Tradition in a battle context; she is born of wrath and epitomizes the fearful, vicious aspects of death and destruction. She is cruel, ferocious, and horrible to look at. She delights in slaughter, and her weird howl and uncanny laughter terrify her enemies. In later Purāṇic and Tantric literature none of her rough edges is smoothed or ignored. In the *Purāṇas*, though, she becomes associated with Śiva and an "established" mythological tradition. As his wife, consort, or even antagonist, she is incorporated into the tradition and, in some cases, becomes identified with a milder dimension of divinity. In the *Tantras* she maintains her fierce aspect but is confronted boldly by the hero, who thus identifies with her, controls her, and wins her boons. In the devotion of Rāmprasād and Ramakrishna, Kālī is addressed as "Mother." Despite her strange appearance and weird behavior, these two Bengali saints saw in her a loving, maternal presence. They saw behind or beneath her ferocity an enduring love. They saw her external appearance as a mask, and by persistently approaching her as children, they succeeded in making her take off that mask.

Several things are clear in the history of the goddess Kālī. First, she does not appear in the texts of the earliest tradition (although she shares many characteristics with the goddess Nirṛti) but appears at a fairly late period in the history of Hinduism. Second, she is associated throughout her history, but particularly in early references, with "peripheral" peoples and cults. She seems to be accepted into the Hindu pantheon reluctantly and gradually. Third, although she came to be most popular in Bengal, she seems to have been known at a very early period throughout India and very early was associated with the Vindhya Mountains (South-Central India) in particular. Fourth, her appearance changes, softening to some extent, as she becomes known as a central deity in Tantrism and Bengal devotionalism.

The Sword: Kālī, Mistress of Death

Who Kālī is, what her "taming" means, and what themes underlie the vision she expresses—questions I have only alluded to thus far—are treated directly in Chapter IV.

CHAPTER IV

Introduction

Several ways of interpreting the significance of Kālī have been suggested by scholars in the past, and it is perhaps worthwhile to review these briefly before suggesting my own. Kālī's association with Bengali nationalism, particularly at the time of the 1905 partition, has been used as evidence to support a theory that she is to a great extent a Bengali goddess personifying aspects of the Bengali character.[1] This theory is strengthened by Kālī's current popularity in Bengal and her fairly old associations with that part of India. There is no denying that Kālī on several occasions has been interpreted by the Bengalis as the symbol or personification of their motherland. The following quotation from the nationalistic Bengali journal *Yagantar* (from around 1905), for example, invites its readers to throw out the British in Mother Kālī's name:

> Rise up, rise up, O sons of India, arm yourselves with bombs, despatch the white *Asuras* [demons] to Yama's abode [Yama is the lord of death]. Invoke the Mother Kali; nerve your arm with valour. The Mother asks for sacrificial offerings. What does the Mother want? The cocoanut? No. The fowl or a sheep or a buffalo? No. She wants many white *Asuras*. The Mother is thirsting after the blood of the Feringhees [foreigners] who have bled her profusely. Satisfy her thirst. Killing the Feringhee, we say, is no murder. Brother, chant this verse while slaying the Feringhee white goat [Kālī is normally only offered black goats], for killing him is no murder: With the close of a long era, the Feringhee Empire draws to an end, for behold! Kali rises in the East.[2]

[1]Ernest A. Payne, *The Śāktas* (Calcutta: Y.M.C.A. Publishing House, 1933), pp. 100–104. For further discussion of Bengali nationalism following the partition of Bengal in 1905, see Al. Carthill, *The Lost Dominion* (Edinburgh: William Blackwood & Sons, 1924), and Valentine Chirol, *Indian Unrest* (London: Macmillan & Co., 1910).

[2]Cited in Chirol, *Indian Unrest*, p. 346.

Well before partition in 1905 the Bengali novelist Bankim Chandra Chatterjee had suggested Kālī as a personification, or representation, of Bengal in his novel *Ānandamath.* The story is about a militant band of holy men who try to throw off the yoke of Muslim rule in Bengal in the period around 1773, when such a revolt actually did take place. The political message of the novel, however, was easily applicable to the times in which it was written (late nineteenth century). In one passage, during which the hero of the story, Mahendra, is being shown around the secret temple of the militant *sannyāsins*, an image of Kālī is described, hidden away in a dark, underground chamber. As Mahendra gazes on her terrible form in the gloom of the chamber, the monk tells him that this is what Bengal has now become. She is now a land of death, poor, with no clothes. He is told further that the girdle of arms around her waist is made of the arms sacrificed to the Mother by her children in her defense.[3]

While it is impossible to deny Kālī's connection with Bengali nationalism, and with Bengal generally, it is possible, I think, to overemphasize its importance. It is certainly nothing new to see religion serving political ends, and it is not surprising at all that Kālī, whose appearance and reputation are terrifying, was used by some Bengalis as a symbol of Bengal or of Bengali resistance during periods of political strife. What should not be forgotten, however, is that Kālī is well known outside Bengal, too, and that within Bengal itself other deities were used in the same way. Indeed, Chatterjee's "Bande Mātaram" ("Hail to the Mother"), a song used as a national anthem in Bengal during the late nine-

[3]Bankim Chandra Chatterjee, *The Abbey of Bliss*, trans. Nares Chandra Sen-Gupta (Calcutta: Padmini Mohan Neogi, n.d.), pp. 39–41. It is interesting to note that the *sannyāsins*, the nationalist heroes of this novel, are all Vaiṣṇavas, worshipers of the demon-slaying Viṣṇu, and not Śāktas (p. 101). In Chatterjee's novel several other goddesses also represent Bengal, however, notably Durgā, Sarasvatī, and Lakṣmī. Kālī represents Bengal only in its downtrodden condition.

teenth and twentieth centuries, has no specific allusion to Kālī at all in its description of Mother Bengal, although "Durgā," "Sarasvatī," and "Lakṣmī" are all given as her epithets.[4] I am inclined to think, then, that any interpretation of Kālī that seeks to stress her essential nature as a personification of Bengal falls wide of the mark in locating her significance in the Hindu tradition.

Another interpretation of Kālī focuses not so much on the Bengali people as on Bengal's climate and the pitiable circumstances of the Bengali peasant that put him at the mercy of Bengal's unpredictable, capricious weather. After describing the plight of Bengal's peasants and the catastrophic effects of a cyclone, Ernest Payne writes:

> The life of the ordinary Bengal peasant must have been a hopeless and helpless one, and it is not difficult to understand his seeking refuge in a conception of the divine as destruction, in a deity unreliable, irresponsible almost, dancing a mad dance of death, and propitiated only by cruel rites and degrading practices.[5]

It might also be noted in support of this interpretation that Kālī is associated with various diseases and is often propitiated during epidemics in Bengal. While there is certainly some basis for such an interpretation of Kālī's popularity in Bengal, it must not be forgotten that she is known throughout India and that her nature cannot be reduced to caprice, whether manifested in nature or in disease. Given her other associations, notably with death, and her terrifying aspect, it is not surprising that Bengalis should see in natural catastrophe and epidemics the manifestations of Kālī. This is not to say, though, that Kālī may be explained as a personification of these things—that she is the creation of helpless, suffering Bengali peasants. There is something more fun-

[4]See Payne, *The Śāktas*, p. 102, for this hymn.

[5]Ibid., pp. 86–87.

damentally Hindu and more fundamentally human about the vision of Kālī than this interpretation suggests.

Somewhat similar interpretations of Kālī, both of them in a clearly Jungian vein, are offered by Erich Neumann and Heinrich Zimmer. Neumann interprets Kālī, and every other terrifying goddess, as a manifestation of the archetype of the Great Mother. In the maturation process the psychic end of man for Neumann is the development of a strong, independent ego. There are various obstacles that inhibit this development, however. One of the most formidable, according to Neumann, is the overweening and overbearing mother, the mother who refuses to allow her child any freedom, who completely inhibits him from exercising self-reliance and smothers him, crippling and killing his developing ego. The archetype expressive of this aspect of the maturation process is the Great Mother, whose youthful consort is weak and effeminate. In her fierce aspect she reveals herself for what she is, the terrifying mother who destroys the ego. Seen from the ego's point of view, however, there is inherent redemption in this aspect, for revealed as she really is she no longer attracts the ego by her smothering warmth but repells it, making it ready to progress to full maturity.[6]

For Zimmer the Goddess generally represents a return to childhood and nonindividuality. It is a rejection of "manliness," conquest, individual achievement, and exertion of the ego. It is the "homecoming of the small child," "the spiritual clutching of the babe."[7] In Zimmer's view Rāmprasād's (and to some extent Ramakrishna's) devotion to Kālī is childishly meek, petulant, and naïve. Rāmprasād's devotion not only reveals a regression but, worse, reveals his ignorance of who Kālī really is. For

[6]Erich Neumann, *The Origins and History of Consciousness,* trans. R. F. C. Hull (New York: Harper & Bros., 1962), 1:39–101; Neumann, *The Great Mother*, trans. Ralph Manheim, 2d ed. (New York: Pantheon Books, 1963), especially pp. 147–72.

[7]Heinrich Zimmer, "Die Indische Weltmutter," *Eranos Jahrbuch* 6 (1938): 213.

Kālī (and the Goddess generally) gives no mercy, bestows no comfort. She represents the inevitables of life—birth, growth, decay, death, and pain. As such she cannot be merciful. To plead for her comfort and to beg her boons is naïve, a fundamental rejection of man's spiritual destiny— *nirvāṇa* (or *mokṣa*)— which is won only by the heroic striving of the mature man. She cannot bestow release (because of what she is); she can only provoke the quest for release by revealing to the spiritual adept life as it really is. To think otherwise is to succumb to the archetypal obstacle of the Great Mother.

> *Nirvāṇa* is the opposite of the mother-child relationship. The mother continually gives birth, always makes way for the new, the vital. She lets her countless sons play their games of heroic conquest, but then impartially consumes them all with her countless tongues, for she is Life (which also must die). The conqueror of *nirvāṇa*, though, no longer dances to her magic, irresistible pulses. He has gone through to oblivion, never to enter the throb of life again. For those still left within her orb, release can be obtained, though, and it may be obtained by concentrating on her very image. The uncompromising idea of mother-love and mercilessness can provoke a man to release.[8]

The weakness of this interpretation, especially as articulated by Neumann, is obvious. In an attempt to exegete Hindu mythology, another mythology has been offered as a key, the somewhat parochial, Western, male-chauvinist myth of individual assertiveness as expressive of the redeemed man (or the psychologically healthy man). Unless we can presuppose the truth of the Jungian interpretation of the maturation process and the mythology of the archetypes that expresses this process, the interpretation must be questioned. Zimmer's interpretation is more attractive, particularly insofar as he is less reductionistic in his use of Jungian mythology. His interpretation, unlike Neumann's, is articulated with reference to Indian spiritual concepts, which somewhat

[8]Ibid., p. 219.

obscures his use of Jungian psychology. On the positive side, both interpretations seek to come to terms with the central ambiguity of Kālī: the ambiguity of the terrifying, ferocious mother.[9] Neither interpretation, however, does justice to the redemptive actualities of devotion to the dread goddess. To interpret this devotion as naïve or regressive seems to me to betray a lack of understanding of Kālī that is grounded in an unnecessarily narrow view of both her and her devotees. Or, perhaps, it might be more accurate to say that this view (particularly Zimmer's rendition) betrays a cynicism, a fundamental distrust of all those who claim to have in fact received the Mother's boon. To accept this interpretation is to call into question most of Ramakrishna's spiritual odyssey, to suggest that this typical and very popular Hindu saint was mistaken, misguided, or deluded. There are other interpretations that do not necessitate such a conclusion.

In suggesting my own interpretation of Kālī I do not want to give the impression that I completely reject the above interpretations. Religious myths and symbols are extremely complex things, the meanings of which are almost always multivalent. Interpretations, in the final analysis, usually fall short of exhausting such phenomena. I have suggested that the above interpretations are reductionistic. This in itself, of course, is not a valid criticism. There is certainly no harm, and much of a positive nature, in demonstrating the sociopolitical, climatic, or psychic implications of Kālī.

To suggest that Kālī may be entirely understood from any of these points of view, however, is unfair and misleading. It is unfair and misleading, as I suggested in the Introduction, because it does not seek to interpret Kālī on her own plane of

[9]It is precisely this ambiguity that is ignored in recent allegorical and rationalistic interpretations of Kālī that appear periodically (usually around Kālī Pūjā day) in the Bengal press. For some examples of this kind of interpretation, see Constance Kapera, *The Worship of Kali in Banaras: An Inquiry* (Delhi: Motilal Banarsidass, n.d.), especially pp. 94–101.

reference. Kālī is a Hindu goddess; she is a being who has revealed herself to the Hindu tradition and whose popularity suggests that she typifies in some way the Hindu vision of the divine. In trying to understand Kālī, the place to begin, it seems to me, is with a consideration of the Hindu vision of reality and the ways in which Kālī either embodies elements of this vision or dramatically illustrates them. It is clear to me that Kālī does, in fact, express several central Hindu themes, and it is by articulating what those themes are and how she expresses them that I will try to offer an interpretation of the dark goddess.

Kālī as Mahāmāyā

A central theme in Hindu spirituality is the idea of *māyā*. Essentially *māyā* is what prevents man from seeing the world as it really is. It is grounded in "not-knowing" *(avidyā)* and is said to be the result of superimposition. Man, in his ignorance, superimposes various structures and images upon things as they really are, thus preventing true "seeing." In his state of not-knowing, man comes to see the world as permanent, pleasant, and worthy of his ultimate attachments. He also sees it as dual, fractured into bits and pieces, something "out there" to which he must respond and react continually. *Māyā*, therefore, both lures man into a false sense of security and reality and clutters and fragments his picture of reality.

Māyā may be understood from another point of view. In this view *māyā* is seen as the extraordinary power of the gods. Throughout Hindu mythology the gods are said to be *māyins*, great magicians who conjure the worlds into existence effortlessly. Śiva, for example, dances the worlds into being, while Viṣṇu dreams them into existence as he reclines upon the cosmic serpent Ananta. Spontaneously, sometimes playfully, the great Hindu gods create and destroy worlds like cosmic wizards. The worlds created by the gods, particularly this world of ours, have a phantasmagoric quality about them. The worlds are like (or, indeed, are) ephemeral, magical creations, dazzling to the senses but ultimately as insubstantial as images in a dream.

From either point of view the spiritual intention of the idea of *māyā* is the same. The world, either as the creation of man's not-knowing or as the dazzling creation of the gods, is of only contingent reality. The lesson of *māyā* for the person who would strive for *mokṣa* or enlightenment is that the world finally must be seen for what it is, a fleeting, constantly changing, magical creation of the mind or the gods. The lesson of *māyā* is that the spiritual adept must be able to see beyond or through things as they appear to things as they really are. The lesson is that the spiritual hero must tear the veil of *māyā* before confronting fully and completely his true self or the divine in its fullness. From either point of view the goddess Kālī illustrates the idea of *māyā* or the religions implications of knowing the world to be essentially *māyā*.

Ramakrishna once had a vision of *māyā*. In this vision he saw a beautiful young woman, pregnant and about to give birth, emerging from the Ganges. She lay down on the bank and soon gave birth to a son. She suckled him and caressed him fondly. Suddenly she was transformed into a terrible hag. She grasped the infant, crushed him in her mighty jaws, and returned into the waters of the Ganges.[10] The world of "my" and "me" is alluring, bewitching, and fleetingly beautiful. For him who sees truly, however, such a world is seen as a narrow, binding, petty world of self-centeredness. The man who truly sees has torn the veil of *māyā*; he is able to focus on the flux of all things, the inevitable decay of sensual beauty, the futility of worldly security. He is able, that is, to discern the shrew who lurks behind the beautiful mask.

Kālī quite clearly conveys *māyā* as seen from the "other shore." She illustrates strikingly what the world of appearance looks like

[10]M., *Gospel of Ramakrishna*, pp. 21–22.

to the one who has seen beyond. She may be voluptuous and smiling in her later representations, suggesting the dark allure of the world based on not-knowing, but her overall presence, which is frightening, and her dwelling place in the cremation ground clearly mock the ultimate significance of a world grounded in the ego. For the pilgrim who has crossed to the other shore, who has torn the veil of *māyā*, the world left behind or transcended is revealed in all its pretense. With awareness grounded in knowledge, the enlightened one is able to focus on the cremation ground as the end of worlds grounded in a grasping ego. The one who sees truly no longer superimposes false and superficial images on the world as it is but rather focuses on the unmistakable reality of the world as painful and fleeting.

Kālī, of course, not only represents the world of *māyā* seen from the other shore of enlightenment. She also acts as a catalyst to one who strives to reach the other shore, who strives to see truly. This is quite obvious when she is seen as embodying *māyā* itself from the second point of view.

Kālī is a particularly appropriate image for conveying the idea of the world as the magical creation of the divine. The world as the play of the gods, the spontaneous, effortless, dizzying creation of their divine reflex, is conveyed in her wild appearance. In her mad dancing, disheveled hair, and eerie howl there is made present the hint of a world reeling, careening out of control. Insofar as Kālī reflects the phenomenal world, or is identified with the phenomenal world, she presents a picture of that world that underlines its ephemeral, unpredictable, spontaneous nature. For Kālī is said to be mad. She is out of control, just as the usually measured and stately rhythms of Śiva's dance sometimes get out of control and destroy the world or as Viṣṇu's dreams sometimes border on nightmares, as when his first "dreamed" creatures (Madhu and Kaiṭabha) seek to destroy the dreamer himself. If Kālī is mistress of this world, as she is frequently said to be, then this world of hers is an insane asylum. With her equally mad and wild lord, Śiva, Kālī reigns over and impels onward the dizzying creation that is this world.

> Crazy is my Father, crazy my Mother,
> And I, their son, am crazy too!
> Shyama [the dark one, meaning Kālī] is my Mother's name.
> My Father strikes His cheeks and makes a hollow sound:
> *Ba-ba-bom! Ba-ba-bom!*
> And my Mother, drunk and reeling,
> Falls across my Father's body!
> Shyama's streaming tresses hang in vast disorder;
> Bees are swarming numberless
> About Her crimson Lotus Feet.
> Listen, as She dances, how Her Anklets ring![11]

Kālī is mad, or at least intoxicated, for, as Ramakrishna puts it so pointedly: "Who would create this mad world unless under the influence of divine drunkeness?"[12] She is the mad mistress of a mad world, a world that is mad with self-intoxication and that is plummeting unknowingly to its own destruction.

Meditation upon Kālī as an image of this world calls into question the stability, order, and destiny of the phenomenal world. Confronted with the reality of a world either as embodied by Kālī or as ruled by Kālī, one is compelled to question seriously a vision of the world as dependable, stable, and predictable. There is a chaotic dimension to the world, an unpredictable, frightening "other" dimension to this world that undercuts attachments to it. Kālī confronts one with a vision of the world as chaotic and out of control and thereby urges one to see beyond it to what is permanent and eternal. In this sense Kālī is both the embodiment or mistress of this ephemeral, magically created world and the stimulus to resolve to transcend it. She depicts

[11]Ibid., p. 961. Kālī's madness is a consistent theme in the songs of Rāmprasād. See, for example, ibid., p. 516, and Thompson and Spencer, trans., *Bengali Religious Lyrics, Śākta*, no. 23, pp. 45–46.

[12]M., *Gospel of Ramakrishna*, p. 13.

the nature of *māyā* in such an unambiguous way that one is able to see the world as it really is and therefore be repelled by it.

Kālī as Prakṛti and Duḥkha

Kālī also illustrates the truths underlying the ideas of *prakṛti* and *duḥkha*, two other themes central to Indian spirituality. *Prakṛti* is sometimes referred to as primordial or elemental matter. *Prakṛti* is matter, but it also pertains to aspects of reality that we understand to be immaterial, such as the mind and the ego. It is more than matter, more than the physical phenomenal world; it is also the inherent urge, the driving force that impels matter to multiply and diversify into increasingly grosser forms. *Prakṛti* is the blind, persistent flow of things within the phenomenal world toward individuality and satisfaction of the ego. It dictates that a man's perception will be oriented outward, grasping, aggrandizing, seeking to arrange the world in such a way that he is at its center. *Prakṛti* is never still, for *prakṛti* is life and the thirst for life. Unchecked, *prakṛti* careens along on a rampage of blind creativity, completely obscuring the underlying unity and reality of the world. Unchecked in man, *prakṛti* blinds him to his essential nature and leaves him spiritually impotent, completely intoxicated with his physical needs and surroundings, incapable of undertaking the spiritual rigors of the *yogin's* heroic inward pilgrimage, which is necessary for discoverings one's essential nature as a spiritual being.

Kālī is a dramatic illustration of *prakṛti's* irresistible, blind, topsy-turvy, insatiable stampede to multiply into grosser and grosser manifestations of matter. Kālī's mad, tumultuous dancing, as Māṇikka Vāchakar suggests, may be seen as expressing the entire world subject to the violent agitation of *prakṛti* gone out of control in its reckless rush to fulfill its innate urge. Wild and uncivilized, Kālī represents the possibility of a world completely overcome by intoxication with the sensual and the physical.

She is the jungle, lush and voluptuous in her nudity, untamed, uncultured, uncaring, and uncompromising in her ongoing struggle to survive and grow. Living on the periphery of civilization, she threatens to invade and destroy it, threatens to overgrow it or trample it in her mad dance of life and death. She is preeminently the goddess who is served with blood, who is pleased with blood, who subsists on blood. Her force and power reside in the hot, pumping blood of all creatures—she is reinvigorated when the blood of birth is returned to her in the blood of death. She sustains life and is herself sustained by the giving back of life. An eighteenth-century icon of Kālī gruesomely depicts her as the all-sustaining and all-consuming substratum of life. She is utterly terrible to look at. Her face is fierce, her stomach is sunken, and her arms and legs are skeletal. She cups one of her breasts in her hand, suggesting her life-giving power. She squats on a corpse and with her other hand feeds herself on her victim's intenstines.[13] She is described elsewhere, in a Tantric text, as follows:

> She is standing in a boat that floats upon an ocean of blood. The blood is the lifeblood of the world of children that she is bringing forth, sustaining, and eating back. She stands there and sips the intoxicating warm blood-drink from a cranial bowl that she lifts to her insatiable lips.[14]

The First Noble Truth of the Buddha is, "All is suffering [*duḥkha*]," a truth that the Hindu tradition, too, has assumed for most of its history. What the Buddha articulated in his formula and what *duḥkha* means to the Indian tradition is not simply that life has its misfortunes, bad luck, or tragedies. *Duḥkha* suggests something much more fundamental in Indian spirituality: it underlines the inevitable realities of sickness, old age, and death, the inevitable change and passing away of things. For

[13]Heinrich Zimmer, *Myths and Symbols in Indian Art and Civilization*, ed. Joseph Campbell (New York: Harper & Row, 1962), plate 68.

[14]Ibid., p. 213.

Buddhism, and to a great extent for Hinduism as well, the first step in man's spiritual quest is meditation on this point: sickness, old age, and death are the very texture of life, and to think otherwise is to remain hopelessly deluded. To live is by definition to participate in these realities. This is the way things are, and nothing can be done to change it.

In a less linear, less formalized way, Kālī conveys the same truth. The image of Kālī in the cremation ground or as a shrunken, wrinkled, skeletal hag fastens one's attention on those aspects of life that cannot be avoided and must eventually result in pain, sorrow, and lamentation. As illustrative of *māyā* and as the embodiment of uncaring, pulsing *prakṛti*, Kālī forces man's attention upon those aspects of life that cannot be kept at bay or successfully repressed. She is the mythological embodiment of those three "passing sights" that provoked the Buddha himself to abandon the world in search of enlightenment, those same sights that are presupposed in his First Noble Truth: sickness, old age, and death.

Kālī as Time

Another important aspect of Hindu spirituality is the concept of time as infinite and cyclical. Time has no beginning and no end, and history repeats itself eternally. According to the Hindu view of time, each world cycle is divided into four *yugas: kṛta* (1,728,000 years), *tretā* (1,296,000 years), *dvāpara* (864,000 years), and *kali* (432,000 years). Each *yuga* diminishes in length of time, as each represents a decline in virtue. The mythical cow representing *dharma* stands on four legs during the *kṛta yuga*, three during the *tretā yuga*, two during the *dvāpara yuga*, and on only one leg during the *kali yuga*, the age in which we are now entangled and in which morality and virtue are at an ebb. Each cycle of four *yugas* is known as a *mahāyuga* and comprises 4,320,000 years. One thousand *mahāyugas,* or 4,320,000,000 years, is equal to one day of Brahmā, or one *kalpa*. Each day of Brahmā sees the creation of the world and each night (equal in time to one day of Brahmā), its dissolution. But even this incredible span of time is made insignificant when we learn that there is an even greater cycle that revolves around the lifetime of Brahmā. Brahmā lives for one hundred Brahmā years of Brahmā days and nights (4,320,000,000 × 2, × 365, × 100), or for the incredible time of 311,040,000,000,000 human years. And at the end of his lifetime all things become totally dissolved including Brahmā himself. Then, for a Brahmā century nothing exists but primeval substance. At the end of this time, the great cycle begins again and, we may assume, continues endlessly.[15]

Time in this view ultimately reduces to insignificance even the most monumental of man's worldly achievements. This cosmic, cyclical view of time underlies the truth of the Indian verse: "A thousand years a city, a thousand years a desert." And time also reduces to the banal all we treasure as unique. Individual biographies in this cosmic view of time are simply brief scenes in an endless drama of lives, perhaps even "repeats" lived countless times in the past.

Kālī, the terrible, the remorseless, conveys superbly this truth of the tradition. For Kālī, too, who is frequently called the Mistress of Time (and whose name may be translated as the feminine form of "time," *kāla*), is that being or force who wears all things down. As Sister Nivedita says, "Her mass of black hair flows behind Her like the wind, or like time, 'the drift and passage of things.' "[16] Her lolling tongue dramatically depicts the fact that she consumes all things. Her appetite is unquenchable, and she is utterly undiscriminating. All things and all beings must yield to relentless, pitiless grinding down by the Mistress of Time. Kālī lives in the cremation ground, mocking distinctions

[15]Zimmer, *Myths and Symbols,*, pp. 13–19.

[16]Sister Nivedita [M. E. Noble], *Kali the Mother* (Mayavita, Almora, Himalayas: Advaita Ashrama, 1953), p. 33.

of class and caste, rich and poor, success and failure. All, in the end, are consumed in her undiscriminating fires. The frantic strivings and hectic yearnings, the carefully cultivated social relationships and impassioned familial and erotic ties end in her fires. As eternal, remorseless time she confronts man with the pitifully finite nature of meanings and attachments based on an individual biography.

Meditation on Kālī, confrontation of her, even the slightest glimpse of her, restores man's hearing, thus enabling or forcing a keener perception of things around him. Confronted with the vision of Kālī, he begins to hear, perhaps for the first time, those sounds he has so carefully censored in the illusion of his physical immortality: "the wail of all the creatures, the moan of pain, and the sob of greed, and the pitiful cry of little things in fear."[17] He may also be able to hear, with his keener perception, the howl of laughter that mocks his pretense, the mad laugh of Kālī, the Mistress of Time, to whom he will succumb inevitably despite his deafness or his cleverness.

Confrontation and Acceptance of Death: Kālī's Boon

My Mind, why so fretful, like a motherless child? Coming into the world you sit brooding, shivering in the dread of death. Yet there is a Death that conquers death, the Mightiest Death, which lies beneath the Mother's Feet. You, a serpent, fearing frogs! How amazing! What terror of death is this in you, the child of the Mother-Heart of all? What folly is this, what utter madness? Child of that Mother-Heart, what will you dread? Wherefore brood in vain sorrow?[18]

Kālī's association with *māyā*, *prakṛti*, suffering, and time, with the ephemeral, phenomenal world of flux, pain, and sorrow, is epitomized in her association with death. It is impossible to

[17]Ibid., p. 34.

[18]Thompson and Spencer, trans., *Bengali Religious Lyrics, Śākta*, no. 42, p. 57.

review the history of Kālī or meditate upon her image without making this association. Although she has an impressive mythology centering around the battlefield (itself a field of death), it is well known that she prefers above any other place the cremation ground. Her companions are jackals and hideous female ghouls. On her public worship day in Bengal her image is set up in cremation grounds and there worshiped by her devotees. There is nothing subtle about Kālī's identification with death; it is underlined in her mythology, iconography, and worship. In any meaningful interpretation of this dark goddess her association with death must receive primary consideration. She was and still is associated with cults and peoples peripheral to Hindu culture, she has been seen, at certain times, as the embodiment of Bengal, her association with Durgā and Śiva is notable, and she clearly suggests or illustrates certain Hindu religious ideas such as *māyā*, *prakṛti*, and time. All these associations help us in understanding the meaning and popularity of Kālī. Her specific association with death, however, is so clear and sustained that it is difficult to avoid basing any interpretation of Kālī on this notable fact.

Taking Kālī's clear identification with death as central, a rather obvious conclusion seems in order. Insofar as Kālī has come to achieve an important place in the Hindu pantheon, we may conclude that the Hindu tradition has affirmed in some important way the efficacious or spiritually enlightening effect of confronting or meditating upon death.[19] To worship the dark goddess, to meditate upon her terrifying presence, to invoke her name in the cremation ground is, it seems clear, to confront the painful, sorrowful dimensions of the world that are summed up in death. Why is this efficacious in the Hindu milieu? What is the boon of the black goddess that derives from confronting her or serving her feet?

[19]This is also true of Buddhism. See Edward Conze, *Buddhist Meditation* (London: George Allen & Unwin, 1956).

Quite obviously the boon granted to him who confronts Kālī, as already suggested, is that of seeing things as they really are and the consequent tendency or ability to see beyond the finite destiny of an ego-centered life. Indian spirituality has consistently emphasized the truth that man's essential nature is eternal, imperishable, and free. If one can summarize in a phrase the general intention of Indian spirituality, it is to gain release *(mokṣa)* from the bondage of *karma* and *saṁsāra*, to break the bonds of finite limitations and participate in the infinite ground of reality, which is imperishable. Insofar as *mokṣa* is understood to be man's ultimate destiny, death is seen to be itself a release, for the fires of the cremation ground consume only the perishable, fleeting aspects of man and bring to an end (for him who has realized his true destiny) the last fetters binding him to the finite world of the phenomenal. To the man who has discovered his eternal destiny, the cremation ground represents the gateway to complete liberation, the final episode in a journey that has, perhaps, encompassed thousands of lives. For the freed man the cremation ground marks the end of a cycle of bondage to grasping and becoming, the gateway to the final transcendence of a way of being that is limited and grounded in not-knowing.

From this point of view Kālī's overall presence may be understood as benign. Her raised and bloodied sword suggests the death of ignorance, her disheveled hair suggests the freedom of release, and her girdle of severed arms may suggest the end of grasping. As death or the mistress of death she grants to him who sees truly the ultimate boon of unconditioned freedom, release from the cycle of *saṃsāra*, release from pain, sorrow, and not-knowing. Her two right hands, the upper making the *mudrā* of "fear not" and the lower making the *mudrā* of granting boons, convey to him who would seek his true spiritual destiny the knowledge that death is only the passing away of the non-essential and the gateway to ultimate freedom. Death is not feared but is seen as a boon. Kālī's dark, menacing appearance does not frighten but attracts one who has seen thc world for what it really is: the ephemeral, phantasmagoric display of superimposition or the magic of the gods, a world fraught with pain and suffering, a world in which all things perish and pass away.

While it is clear that Kālī as the embodiment of death may direct the religious man toward his ultimate destiny of release from *saṁsāra*, while it is clear that Kālī may indicate the gateway to the final dying away and the transcendence of the world of *duḥkha*, which is grounded in not-knowing, it is also clear that among her devotees the here and now is often celebrated and affirmed. In one way or another this is true of both her Tantric devotees and those who approach her simply as devoted children. It seems that Kālī's boon in some way has to do not so much with directing man's vision to liberation after death as to granting liberation before death. It seems that she is religiously efficacious not simply insofar as she scares man into rejecting the physical world by conveying its darker aspects. To her devotees she has also given a playful freedom in this life, painful though she reveals it to be. And this boon of freedom is not, as Zimmer would have it, the boon of ignorance—an ignorance of the way things really are and a childishness based on futile hope. It is a freedom based on release from ignorance, a freedom that comes to one who knows himself to be mortal, a freedom that enables him to revel in the moment, to accept the fullness of life as a gift to be reveled in rather than a curse to be gotten rid of.

Kālī's boon is won when man confronts or accepts her and the realities she dramatically conveys to him. The image of Kālī, in a variety of ways, teaches man that pain, sorrow, decay, death, and destruction are not to be overcome or conquered by denying them or explaining them away. Pain and sorrow are woven into the texture of man's life so thoroughly that to deny them is ultimately futile and foolish. For man to realize the fullness of his being, for man to exploit his potential as a human being, he must finally accept this dimension of existence. Kālī's boon is freedom, the freedom of the child to revel in the moment, and it is won only after confrontation or acceptance of death. Ramakrishna's childlike nature does not stem from his ignorance of things as they really are but from his realization of things as they really are. He is able to revel in the moment, for he knows that to live any other way is a denial of things as they are. To ignore death, to pretend that one is physically immortal, to pretend that one's ego is the center of things, is to provoke Kālī's mocking laughter.[20] To confront or accept death, on the contrary, is to realize a mode of being that can delight and revel in the play of the gods. To accept one's mortality is to be able to act superfluously, to let go, to be able to sing, dance, and shout.[21] To win Kālī's boon is to become childlike, to be flexible, open, and naïve like a child. It is to act and be like Ramakrishna, who delighted in the world as Kālī's play, who acted without calculation and behaved like a fool or a child. To address the one who

[20]To approach Kālī ignoring what she represents is ludicrous and implicitly condemned in this poem by Vivekānanda:

"I am not one of those," he chanted,
"Who put the garland of skulls round
Thy neck,
"And then look back in terror
"And call Thee 'The Merciful' "
"The heart must become a
burial ground,
"Pride, selfishness, and desire all
broken into dust,
"Then and then alone will the Mother
dance there!"

(Sister Nivedita, *The Master as I Saw Him*, 9th ed. [Calcutta: Udbodhan Office, 1963], p. 178.)

[21]Martin Heidegger seems to be saying something similar. "Anticipation [of death] discloses to existence that its uttermost possibility lies in giving itself up, and thus it shatters all one's tenaciousness to whatever existence one has reached" (*Being and Time*, trans. John Macquarrie and Edward Robinson [New York: Harper & Row, 1962], p. 308).

grants this remarkable freedom, this great boon, as "Mother" does not seem at all inappropriate, naïve, or suggestive of spiritual or human regression. Kālī is Mother to her devotees not because she protects them from the way things really are but because she reveals to them their mortality and thus releases them to act fully and freely, releases them from the incredible, binding web of "adult" pretense, practicality, and rationality.

Kālī's "Taming"

With the previous interpretation in mind, Kālī's "taming" or "completion" perhaps may be understood more clearly. Her defeat by Śiva in a dance contest represents the tenacious, relentless, heroic path of the *yogin* who tames or conquers nature *(prakṛti)* by manfully annihilating it, by withdrawing completely from the world, turning his senses inward and achieving isolation from the mad whirl of things. In association with the *yogin* (Śiva), *prakṛti* (Kālī) is curbed, controlled, and tamed. Equilibrium is restored and expressed in the unlikely pair, the detached *yogin*-god and the mad, wild, destructive goddess. Equilibrium is restored or maintained by the violent, "inhuman," stubborn persistence of the yogic path—by the forceful, strenuous, manful dance of Śiva.

Kālī is tamed in Tantric *sādhana* by another kind of hero—the adept who willingly meets her on her own terms and in her own sanctuary, who confronts her in the dead of night in the cremation ground. In confronting the terrible, black goddess, the adept confronts the "forbidden" dimensions of reality by partaking of them. He puts the spotlight, as it were, on those darker, murkier dimensions of his own being. He lets the ghosts and frightening monsters of his instinctual subconscious being emerge into the light, where they are aired, studied, consciously accepted, and hence stripped of their power to bind him. He conquers these hidden monsters by ritually forcing himself to end that instinctual, perceptual censorship that insists on blinding him to the realities of death and pain. By meditating on Kālī in the cremation ground, by surrounding himself with the dead in the place of death, he overcomes the crippling fear that is the real wrath of the goddess. He wins her boon of fearlessness by confronting her heroically in a ritual context that insists on an acceptance of the forbidden. The following hymn of Vivekānanda, a disciple of Ramakrishna's and leader of the Ramakrishna movement during its formative years, articulates the heroic approach of the Tantric hero and also demonstrates that such an approach does not have to occur in a ritual context.

> The stars are blotted out,
> Clouds are covering clouds,
> It is darkness, vibrant, sonant.
> In the roaring whirling wind
> Are the souls of a million lunatics,—
> Just loose from the prison house,—
> Wrenching trees by the roots,
> Sweeping all from the path.
> The sea has joined the fray,
> And swirls up mountain-waves,
> To reach the pitchy sky.
>
> The flash of lurid light
> Reveals on every side
> A thousand, thousand shades
> Of Death begrimed and black—
> Scattering plagues and sorrows,
> Dancing mad with joy,
> Come, Mother, Come!
>
> For Terror is thy name,
> Death is in Thy breath,
> And every shaking step
> Destroys a world for e'er.
> Thou "Time," the All-Destroyer!
> Come, Mother, Come!

Who dares misery love,
And hugs the form of Death—
Dance in destruction's dance,
To him the Mother comes.[22]

For those who lack the heroic nature of the *yogin*, the Tantric hero, or Vivekānanda, Kālī may be "tamed" in another way. She may be tamed by simple, childlike devotion—a devotion that stems from and results from an acceptance of all the things that she represents. Her devotee is he who accepts the truths that she conveys without struggling against them, who does not whimper and whine but revels in life's moment. Her devotee is like Ramakrishna, who laughs and plays with the Mother, secure in both the inevitability of his own death and the obvious importance of affirming the moment. Kālī's boon is not given capriciously or grudgingly but openly to those who unconditionally accept her and what she represents. She is "stingy" with her boon or terrifying in nature only to those who refuse to accept what she reveals; she remains a shrew only to those who would deny her.[23] To those who accept her, like Ramakrishna, she becomes the Mother, or even sometimes the playful child.

To the individual, Kālī reveals things as they really are by expressing the truths inherent in *māyā*, *prakṛti*, *duḥkha*, time, and death, and then she grants her boon of freedom and reveals herself as Mother. To the Hindu tradition as a whole, this may also be the case. The history of Kālī in the Hindu tradition is

[22]Cited in Sister Nivedita, *Kali the Mother*, p. 105. The same theme of heroic confrontation of Kālī is seen in these words of Vivekānanda: "How few have dared to worship Death or Kālī! Let us worship Death! Let us embrace the Terrible, because it is terrible; not asking that it be toned down. Let us take misery for misery's own sake!" (Sister Nivedita, *The Master as I Saw Him*, p. 172).

[23]In the *Lakṣmī-tantra* (VII. 13) Kālī is said to be benevolent and pleasing in her essential nature. However, she is terrible and deathlike to those who are cruel and selfish. Her terrible appearance thus is dependent on the behavior and nature of men.

in many ways also the story of her taming or completion. In the course of her history she ceases to be regarded as simply a peripheral, savage goddess of wild tribes—a goddess of the jungles and mountains—and she acquires attributes that soften and universalize her. In various ways and in particular mythologies, movements, and individuals she reveals herself to be more than a manifestation of non-Hindu, noncivilized barbarians. The tradition as a whole begins to detect the truths it has itself affirmed—it begins to see in Kālī a dramatic presentation of such central Hindu themes as *māyā*, *prakṛti*, *duḥkha*, and *kāla*.

Whether we say that Kālī was reinterpreted by the tradition (these truths being superimposed upon her intially peripheral nature) or whether we say that she revealed herself in her completeness to the tradition, both Kālī and the tradition were changed and enriched. In the hands of the tradition Kālī is tamed, softened, and completed, but in such a way that she never loses her essential nature as a goddess who embodies the eerie, awesome, terrifying, painful dimensions of life—who delights in blood and dances in wild abandon. The tradition, on the other hand, is affected too. Its vision of the divine is at once reinforced and enriched. Those "other" dimensions of the divine, the tumultuous, wild, uncontrollable aspects of the divine that the tradition affirmed in other deities, are elaborated and pushed to extreme lengths in Kālī. Her appearance and mythology, one could say, "completed" the universal character of the Great Goddess in classical and medieval times by adding to it the dark, terrible aspects of reality that the Goddess represents as life itself. In summary, it could be said that the tradition completed Kālī by taming or softening her, while Kālī completed or enriched the tradition by adding to it a dimension of realism, by providing it with a striking vision of things as they really are.

THE SWORD AND THE FLUTE: CONCLUSION

> Mother with dishevelled hair has world-charming
> beauty; so I love Her black complexion.
> The virtue of black complexion is well-known to
> Śuka, Śiva, gods and sages.
> Śiva, Lord of gods, meditates on Her black complexion in His heart.
> Black complexion is the life of Vṛndāvana, and
> makes the milkmaids indifferent to the world.
> Kṛṣṇa wearing a garland of wild flowers with a
> flute in hand becomes Kālī with a sword.
>
> . . . .
>
> Prasāda says, "When the knowledge of non-difference
> dawns, black forms blend with one another."[1]

I see my Mother, the mad, disordered girl, dancing with gentle movements of her body, now taking up the flute instead of the sword, or again seizing the sword instead of the flute, or yet again at times making both the sword and the flute into one in Her hand; mingling Her laughter with Her dancing; now loosening and now binding up Her hair. If I sleep, she awakens me by coming Herself and playing on the flute. If I commit any offence, She raises Her sword and, smiling gently, threatens me with it.[2]

Kṛṣṇa and Kālī, two of Hinduism's most popular divine beings, seem to present us with two very different visions of the divine. In Kṛṣṇa the divine reveals itself to be irresistibly attractive, overwhelmingly beautiful. In Kālī, however, the divine is perceived as frightening, awesome, and terrible. Kṛṣṇa reveals a world of transcendent joy and bliss; he beckons his devotees to revel with him in Vṛndāvana, where sickness, old age, and death

[1] *Rama Prasada's Devotional Songs*, no. 170, p. 91.

[2] Avalon, ed., *Principles of Tantra*, p. 600.

are not known, where spring is eternal, and where ecstatic love reigns supreme. Kālī's terrifying appearance, on the other hand, calls man's attention to the realities of pain, suffering, and death.

Given the Hindu tradition's affirmation that both deities dramatically articulate certain truths about the nature of the divine, about the nature of a transcendent sphere of reality in which all else is grounded, the first conclusion one is forced to acknowledge is the apparently ambivalent nature of the divine in the Hindu tradition. If both deities reveal the nature of that "other" dimension of reality, the sacred, which the divine participates in and articulates, then the sacred is revealed to be both surpassingly beautiful and sublime and overwhelmingly fierce and terrifying. Taken together, Kṛṣṇa and Kālī seem to affirm in the Hindu context what Rudolph Otto affirms about the Holy in the Judaic-Christian tradition: that is, that the Holy (or the sacred) is at once irresistibly attractive and compelling, on the one hand, and dangerous, frightening, and overwhelming, on the other. In its transcendent mysteriousness the divine discloses two apparently opposite aspects that are dramatically perceived in the images of the beautiful cowherd boy who beckons with his flute and the terrible shrew who threatens with her bloodied, upraised sword.

While it is obvious that Kṛṣṇa and Kālī taken together as representations of the Hindu vision of the divine present very clearly the ambivalent nature of deity, it is also evident that these two extraordinary beings share several characteristics. By focusing on their common characteristics, which are by no means insignificant, it is possible to discover, I think, something fundamental about the Hindu perception of the divine, something beyond the Hindu affirmation of the essentially ambivalent nature of deity, something beyond (or in addition to) the tradition's affirmation that the divine reveals itself in incredibly diverse and rich forms. There is a hint, I think, in the shared characteristics of these two apparently opposite presences of a typically Hindu (or perhaps Bengali) perception of the divine, a hint of some things that are fundamental about the divine in the Hindu context, that persist behind its assortment of masks and disguises. What are these characteristics, then, and what do they suggest about the Hindu vision of the divine?

Certain similarities between Kālī and Kṛṣṇa are clear. They are both black, or dark. What this probably suggests is their tribal, indigenous ancestry. Their color suggests that they are of the land, that their roots go deep, that they are most likely non-Aryan in their origin. The "peripheral" nature of both deities seems to underline this fact. Both Kṛṣṇa and Kālī inhabit the fringes of society. The lovely cowherd Kṛṣṇa, while he is eminently approachable, lives in a cowherd settlement or in the forests of Vṛndāvana. His devotees are not *brāhmans* of the established order, his paradise is far from the artificial din of the city, and his most ardent followers are country women who are called upon to disregard established law and custom by leaving their homes and husbands to revel illicitly with him on the banks of the Jumna. Kālī lurks in the mountains, the jungle, or the cremation grounds on the outskirts of towns and cities. She gains prominence in Tantrism, in many ways an antibrāhmanic system, and is worshiped by wild, uncivilized tribes. Neither deity seems at home in the ordered, hierarchical context of brāmanic society.

There are two important conclusions to be dawn from the peripheral natures of Kṛṣṇa and Kālī. First, what we call the Hindu vision of the divine is grounded in the primordially indigenous soil of India. Kṛṣṇa and Kālī in most essential respects differ from the gods of the *Ṛg-veda*. While they share some minor characteristics with certain Vedic deities, they are strikingly un-Vedic in nature.[3] To generalize about a very complex and varied pantheon, the Ṛg-vedic gods are generally associated with light,

[3]Bhattacharji, as mentioned earlier, tries to show how Kālī is a later development of the Vedic goddess Nirṛti (*Indian Theogony*, p. 85). She also tries to show that

order, harmony, and might and are approached in the context of sacrificial ritual.[4] Kṛṣṇa and Kālī are dark, lush beings associated not with the dazzling light of the heavens but with the blood and sap of the earth, and if they are associated with might and order it is a much more precarious and unpredictable power and order: a power that produces frenzy and madness and an order that is never static in its throbbing rhythms. The Hindu vision of the divine certainly does not forget the truths perceived in the Vedic tradition. The Hindu tradition repeatedly affirms its source as Vedic. But the popularity of Kṛṣṇa and Kālī demonstrates beyond doubt that the Hindu vision of the Real is grounded in another source as well, a source that is the soil of India itself.

The second conclusion to be drawn from the peripheral natures of Kṛṣṇa and Kālī concerns the "otherness' of the divine as perceived in the Hindu vision. The divine reveals itself in Kṛṣṇa and Kālī to be outside or beyond the borders or limitations of ordinary human society and habitation. In this sense the divine is revealed to be other, transcending the human sphere. In approaching the divine, man is called upon to break the bond of established, ordered human existence and participate in a transcendent realm of reality that is essentially untamed.

Beyond similarities of color and ancestry there may be discerned more intrinsic similarities between Kṛṣṇa and Kālī. Both deities betray a hot, voluptuous quality. Kṛṣṇa incites sexual passion in the *gopīs*, driving them to frenzy by his appearance or the call of his flute. He calls the *gopīs* from the staid, humdrum world of order and piety to the topsy-turvy world of the carnival. At the call of his flute the blood boils, and none can resist the summons to

Kṛṣṇa is essentially a sun deity and as such is a derivation or elaboration of the Vedic Viṣṇu.

[4]The Vedic deities that do remind us of Kṛṣṇa or Kālī are usually very minor gods in the *Ṛg-veda*, for example, Nirṛti, Rudra, and Viṣṇu. The only major deity who reminds us of the lush, fertile, intoxicating natures of Kṛṣṇa and Kālī is Soma.

participate in his ecstatic revels. Kālī, too, particularly in her later history, when she is rarely associated with the battlefield, has a warm, voluptuous appearance. She is naked, full breasted, and heavy hipped. She is said to enjoy sexual intercourse with Śiva, taking the "reverse position" in her aggressiveness.[5] She subsists on the hot, rushing blood of all creatures and is frequently shown drinking fresh, steaming blood from a skull bowl. Despite her destructive and terrible features, she is the Mother of all, and as such she reveals a sexually creative presence that is hot and thirsty.

Both deities, furthermore, are associated with strength, vigor, and life: Kṛṣṇa in a consistently affirmative way and Kālī in a negative or ambiguous way. They are both "wet," earthy deities whose presences pervade all species of being. Kṛṣṇa's presence in Vṛndāvana means that spring is eternally present there. Where Kṛṣṇa is, animal and vegetable life is lush, almost jungly.[6] When he plays his flute it sends shudders of delight throughout the entire creation. Trees burst into bloom, and creepers shake loose from trees. Lotuses blossom, and the reeds of the river weep in joy. Where Kṛṣṇa is, or when his flute sounds, the sap of life flows freely and luxuriously. His presence is life, fruitful, bounteous, and wet. Where Kṛṣṇa is, life revels in strength and vigor. His presence is insistently fertile, inciting growth and abundance.

Kālī's dark, voluptuous, bloody presence is similarly "wet." As the great Mother of the world she is portrayed as continually giving birth. Immodest in her nudity and aggressive in her sexuality, she represents the ever fertile womb from which springs the eternal throb of life. She also reveals the flux of life, however —the throb of life gone out of control or the throb of life worn

[5]Kṛṣṇānanda Āgamavāgīśa, *Tantrasāra,* 1:311.

[6]See M. S. Randhawa's *Kangra Paintings of the Gīta Govinda* (New Delhi: National Museum, 1963) and *Kangra Paintings on Love* for pictures portraying the lush sensuality of Vṛndāvana.

out. She is not only the creative source of life but also the dimension of life that untiringly insists on sustenance, satisfaction, satiation. Her lolling tongue, her blood-smeared lips and body, and her bloodied cleaver represent the irreducible truth that life sustains itself on life, that the throb of life—the pulsing beat of rushing blood, the insistent flow of sap—demands an unending stream of life energy to go on, that death and decay form the only fertile ground for the hungry pulse of life. Kālī represents the unrefined, raw, primordial scream of the hungry infant, while at the same time representing the anguished laments of the dying who have exhausted themselves in nourishing and sustaining the next generation. Kālī gives life, unceasingly and fully; she grants her devotee the boon of fertility and birth; but she demands at the same time a continuous flow of fresh blood to sustain her in her ceaseless, maternal efforts.

The conclusion to be drawn from the voluptuous, "wet" natures of Kṛṣṇa and Kālī is that the Hindu vision of the divine is grounded in the irreducible reality of life, in the realities of sex, birth, growth, decay, and death. The divine may reveal itself to be other, to be transcendent and outside the boundaries of human society. But it also reveals itself to be the fundamental ground of all human existence. Strength, vigor, passion—the very sap and blood of life pulse with divine rhythm, expressing and revealing the immediacy and pervasiveness of the divine. The Hindu vision of the divine as articulated in Kṛṣṇa and Kālī affirms that *saṁsāra* is pervaded by the divine, that *saṁsāra*, painful though it may be, is expressive of divine activity. *Saṁsāra* is revealed to be lush, rich, warm, and vigorous. *Saṁsāra* may be essentially māyic in nature, a dazzling, magic show that bewitches, deludes, and ensnares man, but it is also affirmed to be grounded in the warm, redemptive realities of its creators. *Saṁsāra* is to be ultimately transcended, no doubt, but it may be transcended by attuning oneself to its inner rhythms, by learning to dance to the tune of Kṛṣṇa's flute or with Kālī in her dance of creation and destruction. The devotee of Kṛṣṇa or Kālī does not transcend the world by denying it in yogic withdrawal but by dancing to its inner rhythms and thereby participating in its creative and redeeming source.

Kṛṣṇa and Kālī have another similarity. They both betray strains of wildness and frenzy. Even in their historically later, more refined aspects they manifest an untamed quality. Kṛṣṇa's pranks as a child, his tumultuous gambols with his cowherd companions, and his rollicking loveplay with the *gopīs* reveal a being who, if not out of control, is uncontrollable. In Kṛṣṇa that "other" dimension of the divine or transcendent is shown to be unpredictable, intoxicated, and playful. His parents cannot control him, the *gopīs* are helpless when incited to frenzy by his appearance or the sound of his flute, and he himself seems to lose control, intoxicated by the enchanting call of his own flute. He plays and makes love to the *gopīs* with abandon, betraying little or no concern for the maintenance of the world of which he is the Lord. Kālī, too, appears tumultuous and frenzied, acts in wild ways, and is frequently called mad or intoxicated. A repeated mythical theme is the threat she poses to the stability of the world when she dances out of control, intoxicated from drinking the blood of her victims on the battlefield. Her red, glaring eyes, nudity, disheveled hair, and lolling tongue give her an untamed appearance. Her frightening, eerie howl conveys the presence of a primordial wildness that threatens to crash in upon the world, reducing it to chaos.

The wild, frenzied natures of Kṛṣṇa and Kālī suggest the conclusion that the divine in Hinduism is essentially unspecified. The divine represents or embodies unrefined, primordial Being. The peripheral, "jungly," wild nature of these dark beings affirms the truth that the divine cannot be circumscribed. It is totally "other" in its essential nature. Underlying the world of fractured particularity and specificity is a dimension that is completely unbound, primordially free. It is an untamed, fertile dimension from which the world is born and upon which the world rests, a dimension that pervades the world with throbbing life but that threatens to render the world chaotic when it unpredictably changes its rhythm, breaking in on the ordered, artificial routine of citified and civilized man.

The two black gods, finally, also teach the fundamental truth that man in the Hindu tradition is called upon to transcend his limitations as a fettered creature who behaves out of habit. Both beings direct man's vision beyond the limitations of an ego-centered, predictable, humdrum, and deadening existence to an other world that is both terrifying and irresistibly attractive in its transcendence. Kṛṣṇa calls man to dance, sing, and rollick in carnival in his paradise of Vṛndāvana; he calls man to revel in freedom, to give himself up to frenzy, to lose himself hopelessly and helplessly in the bliss of the divine. Kṛṣṇa's bewitching presence releases man to behave with childlike abandon; he enables man to discover that he is inwardly free and unbound, that inwardly he, too, is divine.

Kālī, too, incites frenzy and madness in her devotees. Both Rāmprasād and Ramakrishna were nearly driven mad by appropriating her presence. The flux of the world of the ego having been revealed to them dramatically in the figure of Kālī, they lost their thirst for the things of this world and saw and longed for a transcendent world beyond suffering and death. Participating in that world, they behaved as if mad—intoxicated with and doting upon the wild, black Mother who grants the boon of revealing the world of *saṁsāra* as it really is: fleeting, painful, and finite. In his transcendent vision the devotee of Kālī laughs, sings, and plays, reveling in the Mother's intoxicated creation—affirming his life for what it is, a fleeting episode in Kālī's eternal dance of creation and destruction, a sojourn in *saṁsāra* that may be ultimately redeeming if properly understood. The overpowering, terrible presence of Kālī, revealing the world of *saṁsāra* as fleeting, finite, and painful, invites man to look beyond his temporal existence. She invites man to join in her mad dance in the cremation ground, she invites him to make of *himself* a cremation ground so that she may dance there, releasing him from the fetters of a bound existence. She invites man to approach the cremation ground without fear, thus releasing him to participate in his true destiny, which lies beyond this whirligig of *saṁsāra* in transcendent release.

WORKS CITED

Adigal, Prince Ilango. *Shilappadikaram* [The Anklet Bracelet]. Translated by Alain Danielou. New York: New Directions Book, 1965.

Althaus, Paul. *Mystic Lyrics from the Indian Middle Ages*. Translated by P. Althaus. London: George Allen & Unwin, 1928.

Archer, William G. *The Loves of Krishna in Indian Painting and Poetry*. New York: Macmillan Co., 1957.

Avalon, Arthur [Sir John Woodroffe, ed.] *Principles of Tantra: The Tantratattva of Śrīyukta Śiva Candra Vidyārṇava Bhattacārya Mahodaya*. Madras: Ganesh & Co., 1960.

Banerjee, Asit Kumar. *Bangla Sāhityar Itibritta*. (Bengali.) Calcutta: Modern Book Agency, 1962.

Basava. *Vacanas of Basavaṇṇa*. Edited by H. Deveerappa; translated by L. M. A. Menezes and S. M. Angadi. Sirigere, Mysore: Annana Balaga, 1967.

Basham, A. L. *The Wonder That Was India: A Survey of the Culture of the Indian Sub-continent before the Coming of the Muslims*. New York: Grove Press, 1954.

Behara, K. S. "The Evolution of Śakti Cult at Jajpur, Bhubaneswar and Puri." In Sircar, D. C., ed. *The Śakti Cult and Tārā*, pp. 74–86.

The Bhagavad Gītā. Translated by Franklin Edgerton. New York: Harper & Row, Harper Torchbook, Cloister Library, 1964.

[*Bhāgavata-purāṇa*] *The Srimad-Bhagavatam of Krishna-Dwaipayana Vyasa*. Translated by J. M. Sanyal. 5 vols. 2d ed. (vols. 1, 4, 5); 3d ed. (vols. 2, 3). Calcutta: Oriental Publishing Co., n.d. (2d ed.); 1965 (3d ed.).

Bhandarkar, R. G. *Vaiṣṇavism, Śaivism and Minor Religious Systems*. Varanasi: Indological Book House, [1966].

Bharati, Agehananda. *The Tantric Tradition*. London: Rider & Co. 1965.

Bhaṭṭācārya, Siddheśvara. *The Philosophy of the Śrīmad-Bhāgavata*. Visva-Bharati Research Publication. Santiniketan: Visva-Bharati. Vol. 1: *Metaphysics*, 1960; vol. 2: *Religion*, 1962.

Bhattacharji, Sukumari. *The Indian Theogony: A Comparative Study of Indian Mythology from the Vedas to the Purāṇas*. Cambridge: Cambridge University Press, 1970.

Bhattacharyya, N. N. *Indian Mother Goddess.* Calcutta: R. D. Press, 1971.

Bhavabhūti's Mālatīmādhava with the Commentary of Jagaddhara. Edited and translated by M. R. Kāle. 3d ed. Delhi: Motilal Banarsidass, 1967.

Bolle, Kees W. "Speaking of a Place." In Kitagawa, Joseph M., and Long, Charles H., eds. *Myths and Symbols: Studies in Honor of Mircea Eliade*, pp. 127–39.

Brahma-Vaivarta Puranam. Translated by Rajendra Nath Sen. Sacred Books of the Hindus, vol. 24. Allahabad: Sudhindra Nath Vasu. Part 1: *Brahma and Prakriti Khandas*, 1920; part 2: *Ganesa and Krishna Janma Khandas,* 1922.

Carthill, Al. *The Lost Dominion.* Edinburgh: William Blackwood & Sons, 1924.

Chakravarti, Chintaharan. *Tantras: Studies on Their Religion and Literature.* Calcutta: Punthi Pustak, 1963.

Chatterjee, Bankim Chandra. *The Abbey of Bliss.* Translated by Nares Chandra Sen-Gupta. Calcutta: Padmini Mohan Neogi, n.d.

Chattopadhyaya, Debiprasad. *Lokāyata: A Study in Ancient Indian Materialism.* New Delhi: People's Publishing House, 1959.

Chirol, Valentine. *Indian Unrest.* London: Macmillan & Co., 1910.

Clark, T. W. "Evolution of Hinduism in Medieval Bengali Literature: Śiva, Caṇḍī, Manasā." *Bulletin of the School of Oriental and African Studies* (University of London) 17 (1955): 503–18.

Conze, Edward. *Buddhist Meditation.* London: George Allen & Unwin, 1956.

Coomaraswamy, Ananda K. "Līlā." *Journal of the American Oriental Society* 61 (1941): 98–101.

Das, R. K. *Temples of Tamilnad.* Bombay: Bharatiya Vidya Bhavan, 1964.

Dāsgupta, Śaśibhūsan. *Bhārater Śakti-sādhana o Śākta Sāhitya.* (Bengali.) Calcutta: Sāhitya Saṅgsad, 1367 B.S. [1961].

Dasgupta, Surendranath. *A History of Indian Philosophy.* Vol. 4: *Indian Pluralism.* London: Cambridge University Press, 1966.

De, S. K. *Bengal's Contribution to Sanskrit Literature and Studies in Bengal Vaisnavism.* Calcutta: Firma K. L. Mukhopadhyay, 1960.

———. *Early History of the Vaisnava Faith and Movement in Bengal from Sanskrit and Bengali Sources.* Calcutta: Firma K. L. Mukhopadhyay, 1961.

Works Cited

Devī-māhātmyam: The Glorification of the Great Goddess. Translated by Vasudeva S. Agrawala. Varanasi: All-India Kashiraj Trust, 1963.

Dikshit, S. K. *The Mother Goddess (A Study in the Origin of Hinduism).* Poona: International Book Service, n.d.

Dimock, Edward C. *The Place of the Hidden Moon: Erotic Mysticism in the Vaiṣṇava-sahajiyā Cult of Bengal.* Chicago: University of Chicago Press, 1966.

———, ed. and trans. *The Thief of Love: Bengali Tales from Court and Village.* Chicago: University of Chicago Press, 1963.

Dimock, Edward C., and Levertov, Denise, trans. *In Praise of Krishna: Songs from the Bengali.* Garden City, N.J.: Doubleday & Co., 1967.

Eliade, Mircea. *Yoga: Immortality and Freedom.* Translated by Willard R. Trask. Bollingen Series 56. New York: Pantheon Books, 1958.

Farquhar, J. N. *An Outline of the Religious Literature of India.* Delhi: Motilal Banarsidass, 1967.

Gait, Sir Edward. *A History of Assam.* Revised and enlarged by D. K. Barua and H. V. S. Murthy. 3d rev. ed. Calcutta: Thacker Spink & Co., 1963.

Growse, F. S. *Mathura: A District Memoir.* N.p. : North-Western Provinces & Oudh Government Press, 1883.

Harivamsa. Translated by Manmatha Nath Dutt. Calcutta: Elysium Press, 1897.

Heidegger, Martin. *Being and Time.* Translated by John Macquarrie and Edward Robinson. New York: Harper & Row, 1962.

Hopkins, E. Washburn. *Epic Mythology.* Varanasi: Indological Book House, 1968.

Hopkins, Thomas J. "The Social Teachings of the *Bhāgavata Purāṇa.*" In Singer, Milton, ed. *Krishna: Myths, Rites, and Attitudes,* pp. 3–22.

Hymn to Kālī (Karpūrādi-stotra). Edited and translated by Arthur Avalon [Sir John Woodroffe]. 3d ed. Madras: Ganesh & Co., 1965.

Jaiswal, Suvira. *The Origin and Development of Vaiṣṇavism (Vaisnavism from 200 B.C. to A.D. 500).* Delhi: Munshiram Manoharlal, 1967.

Jayadeva. *The Song of Divine Love (Gita-Govinda).* Translated by Duncan Greenlees. Madras: Kalakshetra Publications, 1957.

Jayānanda. *Caitanya-maṅgala.* Edited by Nāgendra Nāth Basu. Calcutta: Bangīya Sāhitya Pariṣad, 1905.

Jīva Gosvāmin. *Śrīkṛṣṇa-saṁdarbha.* Translated into Bengali by Śrī Pran Gopan Gosvāmin. Navadvīp: Rajani Kanta Nāth, 1332 B.S. [1925].

———. *Śrī Śrī Gopāla-campū.* Translated into Bengali by Rasabihāri Sāṁkhyatīrtha. Murshidabad: published under the patronage of the Rāja of Kasimbazar, Murshidabad, 1317 B.S. [1910].

Kapera, Constance. *The Worship of Kali in Banaras: An Inquiry.* Delhi Motilal Banarsidass, n.d.

Kennedy, Vans. *Researches into the Nature and Affinity of Ancient and Hindu Mythology.* London: Longman, Rees, Orme, Brown & Green, 1831.

Kinsley, David R. "The Divine Player: A Study of Kṛṣṇa-līlā." Ph.D. dissertation, Divinity School, University of Chicago, 1970.

Kitagawa, Joseph M., and Long, Charles H., eds. *Myths and Symbols: Studies in Honor of Mircea Eliade.* Chicago: University of Chicago Press, 1969.

Krishnadas [Charuchandra Guha]. *Krishna of Vrindabana.* Calcutta: Bengal Library Book Depot, 1927.

Kṛṣṇadāsa Kavirāja. *Govinda-līlāmṛta.* Translated into Bengali by Saccidānanda Gosvāmin Bhaktiratna of Navadvīp. Vṛndāvana: printed under the patronage of Banamali Roy and published by Nityasvarup Brahmacārī at Śrī Daivokinanda Press, 1908.

———. *Śrī Śrī Caitanya-caritāmṛta.* (Bengali.) 5 vols. Calcutta: published by Mahoranjan Caudhuri at Sādhana Prakāśanī, 1963.

———. *Sri Sri Chaitanya Charitamrita.* Translated by Nagendra Kumar Ray; revised by Satish Chandra Ray. 6 vols. 2d ed. Calcutta: Nagendra Kumar Ray, 1959.

Kṛṣṇānanda Āgamavāgīśa. *Bṛhat Tantrasārah.* (Sanskrit with a Bengali translation.) 2 vols. Calcutta: Basumatī Sāhitya Mandir, 1341 B.S. [1934].

Lahiri, Bela. "Śakti Cult and Coins in North-Eastern India." In Sircar, D. C., ed. *The Śakti Cult and Tārā,* pp. 34–39.

Lakṣmī-Tantra, A Pāñcarātra Āgama. (Sanskrit.) Edited by Pandit V. Krishnamacharya. Madras: Adyar Library & Research Centre, 1959.

M. [Mahendranath Gupta]. *The Gospel of Sri Ramakrishna.* Translated by Swami Nikhilananda. New York: Ramakrishna-Vivekananda Center, 1942.

Mahābhārata. (Sanskrit.) Edited by Vishnu S. Sukthankar et al. Poona: Bhandarkar Oriental Research Institute, 1933.

Mahalingam, T. V. "The Cult of Śakti in Tamilnad." In Sircar, D.C., ed. *The Śakti Cult and Tārā,* pp. 2–33.

[*Mahānirvāṇa-tantra*] *The Great Liberation (Mahanirvana Tantra).* Translated by Arthur Avalon [Sir John Woodroffe]. 4th ed. Madras: Gancsh & Co., 1963.

Majumdar, P. K. "Śakti Worship in Rājasthān." In Sircar, D. C., ed. *The Śakti Cult and Tārā,* pp. 92–100.

Mallik, Girindra Narayan. *The Philosophy of Vaiṣṇava Religion.* Punjab Oriental Sanskrit Series, no. 14. Lahore: Punjab Sanskrit Book Depot, 1927.

The Mārkaṇḍeya Purāṇa. Translated by F. Eden Pargiter. Bibliotheca Indica: A Collection of Oriental Works. Delhi: Indological Book House, 1969.

Mazumdar, B. C. "Durga: Her Origin and History." *Journal of the Royal Asiatic Society of Great Britain* 38 (1906–7): 355–58.

Misra, Janardan. *The Religious Poetry of Surdas.* Königsberg: University of Königsberg, 1934.

Monier-Williams, Sir Monier. *Brahmanism and Hinduism.* 3d ed. London: John Murray, 1887.

Mukherji, S. C. *A Study of Vaiṣṇavism in Ancient and Medieval Bengal —upto the Advent of Chaitanya (Based on Archaeological & Literary Data).* Calcutta: Punthi Pustak, 1966.

Nābhā Dās. *Bhaktamāl.* Edited by Upendranāth Mukherji; translated into Bengali by Kṛṣṇadās Babaji. N.p.: Basumatī Sāhitya Mandir, 1924.

Nāth, Rādhāgovinda. *Śrī Śrī Caitanya-caritāmṛta Bhumika.* (Bengali.) Calcutta: published by Jatīndra Bimat Caudhurī Guru Library, 1958.

Neumann, Erich. *The Great Mother: An Analysis of the Archetype.* Translated by Ralph Manheim. Bollingen Series, vol. 47. 2d ed. New York: Pantheon Books, 1963.

———. *The Origins and History of Consciousness.* Translated by R. F. C. Hull. Vol. 1. Bollingen Library, vol. 42. New York: Harper & Brothers, Harper Torchbook, 1962.

Nivedita, Sister [M. E. Noble]. *Kali the Mother.* Mayavati, Almora, Himalayas: Advaita Ashrama, 1953.

———. *The Master as I Saw Him.* 9th ed. Calcutta: Udbodhan Office, 1963.

O'Connell, Joseph Thomas. "Social Implications of the Gaudīya Vaiṣṇava Movement." Ph.D. dissertation, Harvard University, Cambridge, Mass., 1970.

Oman, J. C. *The Brahmanas, Theists and Muslims of India.* London: T. Fisher Unwin, 1907.

Ortega y Gasset, José. *Toward a Philosophy of History.* New York: W. W. Norton & Co., 1941.

Payne, Ernest A. *The Śāktas: An Introductory and Comparative Study.* Religious Life of India. Calcutta: Y.M.C.A. Publishing House; London: Oxford University Press, 1933.

Pott, P. H. *Yoga and Yantra: Their Interrelation and Their Significance for Indian Archaeology.* Translated by Rodney Needham. The Hague: Martinus Nijhoff, 1966.

Prabodhānanda Sarasvatī. *Ānanda-vṛndāvana-campū.* (Bengali.) N.p., n.d. [Title page missing; probably published late nineteenth century.]

———. *Vṛndāvana-mahimāmṛta.* Translated into Bengali by Haridās Babaji. Vṛndāvana: Bhagavāndās Babaji, 1936.

Przyluski, J. "The Great Goddess of India and Iran." *Indian Historical Quarterly* 10 (1934): 405–30.

Ramanujan, A. K. "Medieval 'Protestant' Movements." Lecture, Introduction to Indian Civilization, University of Chicago, February 7, 1966.

———, trans. *Speaking of Śiva.* Baltimore: Penguin Books, 1973.

Rama Prasada's Devotional Songs: The Cult of Shakti. Translated by Jadunath Sinha. Calcutta: Sinha Publishing House, 1966.

Randhawa, M. S. *Kangra Paintings of the Gīta Govinda.* New Delhi: National Museum, 1963.

———. *Kangra Paintings on Love.* New Delhi: National Museum, 1962.

Rangaswamy, M. A. Dorai. *The Religion and Philosophy of Tēvāram: With Special Reference to Nampi Ārūrar (Sundarar).* Book 1. Madras: University of Madras, 1958.

Raychaudhuri, Hemchandra. *Materials for the Study of the Early History of the Vaishnava Sect.* Calcutta: University of Calcutta, 1936.

Rūpa Gosvāmin. *Bhakti-rasāmṛta-sindhuḥ.* Translated by Tridaṇḍi Swāmī Bhakti Hṛdaya Bon Mahārāj. Vol.1. Vrindaban: Institute of Oriental Philosophy, 1965.

———. *Dāna-keli-kaumudī.* Translated into Bengali by Rāmanārāyaṇa Vidyāratna. Murshidabad: published by Brājanāth Misra at Rādhā-raman Press, 1339 B.S. [1932].

———. *Laghu-bhāgavatāmrta.* Edited by Śrī Balai Cand Gosvāmin; translated into Bengali by Śrī Pran Gopan Gosvāmin. Calcutta: Śrī Śrī Mahāprabhu Mandir, 1304 B.S. [1897].

———. *Lalitā-mādhava.* Translated into Bengali by Satyendranāth Basu. N.p.: published by Satiścandra Mukherji at Basumatī Sāhitya Mandir, n.d.

Saradananda, Swami. *Sri Ramakrishna, the Great Master.* Translated by Swami Jagadananda. Madras: Sri Ramakrishnan Math, 1952.

Sen, Dinesh Chandra. *History of Bengali Language and Literature.* Calcutta: University of Calcutta, 1954.

Sen, Sukumar. *A History of Brajabuli Literature: Being a Study of the Vaisnava Lyric Poetry and Poets of Bengal.* Calcutta: University of Calcutta, 1935.

Singer, Milton, ed. *Krishna: Myths, Rites, and Attitudes.* Honolulu: East-West Center Press, 1966.

Sircar, D. C. *The Śākta Pīthas.* Delhi: Motilal Banarsidass, n.d.

———, ed. *The Śakti Cult and Tārā.* Calcutta: University of Calcutta, 1967.

———. "Śakti Cult in Western India." In Sircar, D. C., ed. *The Śakti Cult and Tārā,* pp. 87–91.

Somadeva. *The Ocean of Story Being C. H. Tawney's Translation of Somadeva's Kathā Sarit Sāgara (or Ocean of Streams of Story).* Edited by N. M. Penzer. Delhi: Motilal Banarsidass, 1968.

Surdas. "The Poems of Surdas for Advanced Students of Hindi." Edited and translated by S. M. Pandey and Norman H. Zide. Mimeographed. Chicago: South Asia Language & Area Center, University of Chicago, 1963.

Thompson, Edward J., and Spencer, Arthur Marshman, trans. *Bengali Religious Lyrics, Śākta.* Calcutta: Association Press (Y.M.C.A.); London: Oxford University Press, 1923.

The Tibetan Book of the Dead or the After-Death Experiences on the Bardo Plane, according to Lāma Kazi Dawa-Samdup's English

Rendering. Edited by W. Y. Evans-Wentz. London: Oxford University Press, 1960.

Tucci, Giuseppe. *Theory and Practice of the Maṇḍala.* Translated by A. H. Broderick. New York: Samuel Weiser, 1970.

Tuker, Francis. *The Yellow Scarf.* London: J. M. Dent & Sons, 1961.

Vidyāpati. *Love Songs of Vidyāpati.* Edited by W. G. Archer; translated by Deben Bhattacharya. London: George Allen & Unwin, 1963.

———. *The Songs of Vidyapati.* Translated by Subhadra Jha. Banaras: Motilal Banarsidass, 1954.

The Vishṇu Purāṇa. Translated by H. H. Wilson. 3d ed. Calcutta: Punthi Pustak, 1961.

Ward, W. *A View of the History, Literature, and Religion of the Hindoos.* 3d ed., abr. London: Black, Parbury & Allen, 1817.

White, Charles S. J. "Kṛṣṇa as Divine Child." *History of Religions* 10, no. 2 (November 1970): 156-77.

Whitehead, Henry. *The Village Gods of South India.* Calcutta: Association Press, 1921.

Zimmer, Heinrich. *The Art of Indian Asia: Its Mythology and Transformations.* Completed and edited by Joseph Campbell. Vol. 1. Bollingen Series, vol. 39. New York: Pantheon Books, 1955.

———. "Die Indische Weltmutter." *Eranos Jahrbuch* 6 (1938): 175–220.

———. *Myths and Symbols in Indian Art and Civilization.* Edited by Joseph Campbell. Bollingen Library 6. New York: Harper & Row, Harper Torchbook, 1962.

———. *Philosophies of India.* Edited by Joseph Campbell. Cleveland: World Publishing Co., Meridian Books, 1956.